HITTING THE SWEET SPOT

THE CONSUMER INSIGHT WORKBOOK

How Consumer Insights Can Inspire Better Marketing and Advertising

by Lisa Fortini-Campbell, Ph.D.

This book is dedicated to The Barbs.

HITTING THE SWEET SPOT

THE CONSUMER INSIGHT WORKBOOK

First Edition

©1992 by The Lisa Fortini-Campbell Company

All rights reserved. Printed in the USA.

Published by The Copy Workshop

A division of Bruce Bendinger Creative Communications, Inc.

For further information contact:

The Copy Workshop

2144 N. Hudson • Chicago, IL 60614

312-871-1179 FAX: 312-281-4643

Hitting The Sweet Spot:

ISBN: 0-9621415-2-6

The Consumer Insight Workbook:

ISBN: 0-9621415-9-3

Associate Editor: Michael Ritchie

Cover Design: Scott Shellstrom/Bruce Bendinger

Typographic Design: Michael Ritchie/Roy Sandstrom

AUTHOR'S NOTE

The point of this book is a simple one– that all of our marketing efforts, from product design through advertising, are successful only to the extent that they connect with a real, live human being– a consumer.

Finding a way to make your brand connect with your consumer is not always easy. Today, it demands that you go beyond just knowing who your consumer is to something deeper– understanding, respect and empathy.

Today's marketers and advertisers need to see the world through their customers' eyes. When this happens, the result is more powerful, more insightful marketing decisions that improve your effectiveness in today's tougher-than-ever marketplace.

But, too often, that's not what happens. Time and again, we miss connecting with our customers, despite the vast amounts of information we have.

This happens not because the information is bad, or the research technique is faulty, but because it hasn't been *interpreted* to the level of real insight. When we only see the world through a marketer's eyes, people become "heavy users" or "beer drinkers." As a result, marketing and advertising campaigns often fail because the people responsible for them lack an insightful understanding of their consumers.

This book addresses what I believe to be one of the most critical problems in advertising and marketing– a lack of consumer insight. It is a view shared by many in the industry.

It's the goal of this book to help you learn the fundamentals of this increasingly important marketing task.

Before we begin, I want you to know that you've already learned many of the lessons in this book, because you're already a real live human being– just like your customers.

You'll find you have a lot of life experiences to draw on when you do the exercises in this book. Much of what we will talk about is the very stuff of life.

By the same token, even though our subject is marketing and advertising, you'll find some guidelines and insights you can use in everyday life. Hopefully, this book will help you every time you want to persuade your friends, your parents, your co-workers or your children.

1+1=3.

That framework is essentially this: you have to find the insight into your consumer and you have to find an insight into your brand. Then you have to bring those two insights together and, as I like to call it, hit the *Sweet Spot*. When you make that connection, good things happen.

It's greater than the sum of its parts. Consumer Insight + Brand Insight = Sweet Spot.

For reasons of style, consistency and clarity, we're going to capitalize the term as a proper noun– in almost every instance. Sweet Spot.

We're going to spend the rest of this book giving you examples and showing you techniques to discover those insights and make those connections.

This book itself is an example of "consumer insight" and "brand insight" connecting. The title is a good example.

One Book. Two Titles.

When I started writing this book, I called it "Hitting the Sweet Spot," appropriating a popular sports metaphor I've used for years with business colleagues.

But, as we started to talk about the book to the two groups we hoped would buy it, we discovered an important insight of our own. While most marketing professionals understood the metaphor and liked the title, it was clearly an inappropriate title for a college textbook– and this was an equally important market for our "product."

As we looked at alternatives, and talked with our "consumers," it became clear that the more appropriate we made our text book title, the less punch it had in the business section of your local bookstore.

We had two different markets, two different consumers, and we had to adjust our messages accordingly. That's the point of our book– get to know your consumer and then use those insights to make informed marketing decisions.

We solved our little marketing dilemma with two book titles. "The Consumer Insight Workbook," is the title of the book as it's published for students. "Hitting the Sweet Spot," is the title of the trade version.

Both are subtitled "How Consumer Insight Can Inspire Better Marketing and Advertising." Except for the cover, they're the same.

"Data Is" – "Him and Her."

Two stylistic and grammatical comments. First, we will treat the large mass of individual "datum " as a singular noun– *"data."*

Just as all the mediums of advertising have become a larger entity known as media, data has become, commonly, and we believe correctly, used as a singular noun.

We are seldom talking about two or more "datum" as a finite set. Rather, we are usually talking about a mass of "datum" which we call *"data."*

And, how to turn this data into meaningful and usable information is a major theme of this book.

Another stylistic (and social) issue is "him and her." In general, I've alternated– unless the group being referred to was clearly male (beer drinkers) or clearly female (mothers.)

Some Words of Thanks.

Now the part of the book where I thank everybody.

First, I'd like to thank my friend and publisher, Bruce Bendinger, and let you know how much his work is a part of this book. The insight that inspired this book was his; he's worked on every idea and edited the whole thing. A first-time author couldn't ask for a better partner.

And thanks to Lorelei Bendinger, Michael Ritchie, Mairee Ryan and the rest of the staff at The Copy Workshop. Everyday they try to put the principles of this book into practice, getting to know their market with affection and insight and developing products to meet the needs of that market.

Finally, I want to thank Joe Plummer, who has been one of the most important influences on my thinking, not to mention my career, even though we never seem to work in the same city at the same time.

In addition to Joe, there have been many, many other people– creatives, account managers, researchers, media people, teachers and clients who have also formed my thinking in important ways and to whom I will always grateful.

You know who you are. Thanks.

Lisa Fortini-Campbell

About the Author

Lisa Fortini-Campbell is a professor at the Medill School of Journalism at Northwestern University teaching in the Integrated Advertising/Marketing Communications Graduate Program. At Medill, she is responsible for giving the students a foundation in consumer insight, communications theory, integrated marketing communications planning and research methods.

Before joining Northwestern, Dr. Fortini-Campbell spent 10 years working in the advertising industry. She began as an analyst in the Leo Burnett Research Department and then moved to Y&R/Chicago where she served as Research Director.

While at Y&R, she also managed the integrated marketing communications program for the Jacobs Suchard account, an international Swiss-based coffee and confectionery company marketing candy in the U. S. under the Brach's brand name.

Building on that experience, Dr. Fortini-Campbell was named General Manager of the newly opened Chicago office of Hal Riney & Partners, a San Francisco-based advertising agency. During her tenure there, she helped double the billings of the office.

In addition to her teaching at Northwestern, Dr. Fortini-Campbell consults for a variety of clients, working with them to plan marketing strategies and consumer insight training programs. She also runs the AAAA sponsored Institute for Advanced Advertising Studies in Chicago.

Dr. Fortini-Campbell earned a Ph. D. in Mass Communications from the University of Washington in 1980. She holds an M. A. in Journalism and a B. A. in Psychology, both from The Ohio State University.

SECTION III
FROM INSIGHT TO INSPIRATION

SECTION IV
CONSUMER INSIGHT AT WORK

Useful
re: Rsch Site/ non-for'g)

Foreword

RESEARCH DONE RIGHT

By Dr. Joseph Plummer
DMB&B, New York

The marketing ideals of understanding the consumer and the reality of how market research is practiced, rarely match up in today's world. But when they do, the result is usually a big breakthrough.

We all recognize how important insightful knowledge of the consumer is to marketing and advertising. But how often do we sacrifice the needs of our consumers to the needs of our own organizations?

In my many years in this business, I've seen this happen all too frequently.

Unfortunately for all of us, the result is often failure. Ads that don't work. Programs that consumers don't respond to. Sales goals that aren't met. New products launched at huge expense with no real audience.

I believe that the reason the needs of the consumer are so often put aside is the distance that exists between marketing people and their target consumers. Most of the time, we're advertising to people quite different from ourselves.

When we don't make the effort to understand them as well as we should (to put ourselves in their shoes and see the world through their eyes) it's easy to focus on creative awards, media frequencies, statistical significance and "client comfort" instead of on what consumers want and need.

It's the purpose of this book to help every marketing and advertising professional put the consumer back in the center of our thought processes.

This book is about consumer research done the way it should be done today. It's about how to make your marketing and advertising ideas serve the consumer rather than the other way around. It's not so much about technique as about getting your head in the right place.

Lisa shows us that getting to know the consumer is something we can all do, regardless of our job within the team. This book shows us how to use the insights we've gained into our consumers' lives to inspire our work day after day after day.

It shows us how to find the way to motivate every consumer–that spot Lisa calls the Sweet spot.

∞

I first became aware of this book before it was a book.

A few summers ago, I sat down to chat with my old friend Bruce Bendinger. He wanted his publishing company, The Copy Workshop, to put out a book on Account Planning.

Bruce had done his homework (as usual) and he had a start on a summary of the efforts to bring the British approach to Account Planning to American advertising. You'll read the final version in Section IV.

We talked about everything from why Account Planning was probably not the right name, to how we approach it at DMB&B, to how it should be taught in the classrooms of America.

We continued to correspond, and then one day I got a delightful surprise.

4

Bruce had met a good friend, Dr. Lisa Fortini-Campbell, perhaps the leading practitioner of consumer-driven research in the Midwest.

I first met Lisa many years ago when I offered her a job at Leo Burnett. In the course of things, our longest time working together under the same agency roof was at Y&R, where she headed up the Research Department in the Chicago office.

I've always been impressed with her ability to "bring the consumer to the table" at an advertising agency.

Agency people have their own Sweet Spots, and Lisa knew how to make the right connections. She knew how to take marketing data, personal experience and consumer research– and turn it into the magic of insight and inspiration.

As in so many other fields, the pioneers are those who match up intellect and ability with artistry and instinct.

And I was excited at the thought that Lisa would take the things she did so well, and share them in written form with the rest of us.

Well, to make a long story short, Bruce and Lisa agreed to do a book together.

They showed me early drafts of the book, and it hit my Sweet Spot dead center. Actually, they hit it a number of times. So I know you're going to enjoy this book!

For most of you already in marketing and advertising, it won't be the blinding light of revelation– because most good marketers and advertisers already know the sense of what Lisa has to share with you.

Rather, it will be what I call the "oh yes!" where what you always thought you knew and believed is confirmed. And, hopefully, it will help you find ways to build upon that commitment to the consumer in your business.

A Special Message To Students

For the students who read this book, this is how consumer research and analysis ought to be approached. At your schools, you'll find many fine instructors showing you how to look at the numbers and learn the techniques that are important as a starting point.

But here, in this book, I hope you also get a sense of how it ought to *feel*. Because the really good stuff- the insights that get out ahead of everyone, spot the trends, and articulate the unarticulated feelings; insights that put new thoughts into people's heads will always be more than technique and data.

And, whatever changes our business goes through, we will always need the people who can give us the inspiration that helps us find those new ideas.

I hope that some of the students reading this book will choose to be consumer-driven researchers, marketers and communicators. We need you. And we need you to be absolutely exceptional.

Because the easy answers were found quite a while ago.

Today, it's tougher than ever. The consumer market is becoming more complex. Competition is becoming global. Technology is changing the mass media.

Helping businesses understand their customers can be a challenging, stimulating and creative career. I hope that many of you decide to make it your job to bring the consumer into the marketing process.

And, to all of you, I hope that when you're done with this small book, you'll make its lessons as large as life.

Whether it's rolling out that new product or just figuring out how to get our kids to do their homework and turn off the TV, we can all improve the quality of our work life and our home life by becoming better at reading other people, and respecting them for who they are.

Think how many hours and how many days go by without our Sweet Spot being hit even once.

And think how good it feels when someone really understands us and speaks to us with a genuine understanding of who we are.

Not as some statistical model, or something to be manipulated like a marionette in the marketplace, but from one living breathing human being to another– with caring, understanding and shared values.

When our Sweet Spot is hit, it feels good.

And I hope this book finds a few ways to hit yours.

1 INTRODUCTION: THE NEED FOR CONSUMER INSIGHT

"If you can't turn yourself into a customer, you probably shouldn't be in the advertising business at all."

Leo Burnett

We all want to be winners.

Especially those of us in marketing and advertising.

Every marketer around wants to be part of a successful new product idea, package design, retailing concept or marketing program.

Everyone in advertising wants to do the same. Each member of the agency team wants to be part of a winning campaign. One that increases sales, garners awards and maybe even prompts a raise or promotion.

But the chances of that happening seem to get smaller and smaller every day. Today, it's a tougher game to win.

Changing Markets • Changing Media • Changing Consumers

Change, we all know, is a fact of life. But the changes now taking place in the world of marketing are so fundamental and irreversible that they force us to set aside our old assumptions, our hard-won experience and our well-worn rules of thumb.

New Economic Realities. With the shift from an industrial economy to a service economy, life in America will never be the same. Gone is the security of stable markets for manufactured goods. Gone along with it are the stable companies that provided those goods, along with stable employment for

8

their workers. Today, producers and consumers face a new economic order, and it's affecting almost everyone.

For many, real income is declining. For all of us, job security is a thing of the past. We don't necessarily expect that we'll live better than our parents did. There are no guarantees, and certainly no free rides. Not for individuals, and surely not for marketers either.

A fact as simple as the shift from growing markets to mature markets has changed the way we all do business.

If "stability" was the watchword of the Old Order, "flexibility" is the name of today's game. To succeed today, a company must be able to spot an opportunity before anyone else, respond to it immediately, and keep pushing to sustain a competitive edge. If that company doesn't, well, today's marketplace is not very forgiving.

New Technology. Information has exploded all around us, giving consumers more knowledge to (hopefully) make better choices than ever before. But, at the same time, it strains their ability to cope.

We've gone from three television networks, and a few independents, to dozens of cable channels; from the Sears Catalogue to thousands of direct marketers. We can call 800 numbers to order products...and 900 numbers for everything from sports news to medical advice. There are television commercials in schools, talking shopping carts in grocery stores, and computers that call us on the phone (usually during dinner).

Every emerging market has its own magazine as quick as you can say "desktop publishing."

Technology has also increased the pace of the marketing game. Information on competitive successes, retailer reactions and consumer preferences flies through point-of-sale scanners, fax machines and computer link-ups. If your product enjoys a competitive advantage today, you might not have it for long, because your competitor can quickly re-tool or re-train and match you in no time.

Then again, with all that information, how do you know what is important?

More Competition. Speaking of competition, it comes from everywhere– from niche players to global behemoths.

For example, one of the most important recent changes in the marketing mix is the increasing power of the retailer. Once-powerful manufacturers have found themselves at the mercy of very smart discounters, warehousers, category-killers, Every Day Low Pricers, and specialists of every kind. It's a new world. And it's going to stay that way.

Changing Consumers. Ultimately, all of these complex changes affect consumers, and they, in turn, are forced to change as well. Drastically.

Today, as consumers, we have an overwhelming number of product choices, brand choices, retail choices and information choices. In a way, that makes us very powerful. With more and more selections to choose from, marketers have to work harder and harder to secure our business.

But it also makes life tougher. There's more to pay attention to, more to think about. And, seemingly, less time to do it. To cope, people are changing the way they live and buy.

Instead of maximizing their choice in every product category, many people search for only as much information as they need to get by.

Rather than display unflinching loyalty to the brands their mothers used, many flit between several brands, depending upon what's on sale.

Some consumers buy the best, most expensive products in some categories, and the lowest priced, unbranded generic products in others.

In this ever more complex world, every individual is finding his own, individual way to live and cope. It's all a part of the growing diversity of today's marketplace. It makes getting in touch with today's consumer even more difficult, yet all the more important.

And even though many human values are timeless, the way we express those values can change as fast as today's headlines.

The great diversity we see among people in demographics, in lifestyle and in buying strategy means the old-fashioned mass market is truly gone for good. The day of marketing to the individual is close at hand.

The Power of Consumer Insight

In the face of all this change– increasing fragmentation of markets, exploding product and media choices, and increasing competition– most marketers are finding it harder than ever to cope.

One of the first strategies is, simply, to spend more money– i.e., bigger advertising campaigns with production budgets to match, more new products, fancier promotions. But there is no guarantee sales will respond. All too often they don't.

So we spend more. We work harder. And we worry more.

There has to be a better way. And there is. It's based on principles that have been around for quite a while.

Take a quick look at some of the winners in today's marketplace. They're bright "points of light" in marketing that can give us all reason for optimism.

Steve Jobs took Apple Computer from his garage to a force that revolutionized the personal computer business.

Sam Walton, of Wal-Mart, whose company has surpassed Sears as America's largest retailer.

Jan Carlzon directed Scandinavian Airlines from near-death to one of the most successful airlines in the world.

Hal Riney, whose ad campaign for Bartles & Jaymes made a "me-too" product from Gallo the number one wine cooler in the country in six months. The list goes on and on.

We wonder: How did they do it? Was it genius or just luck? What do they have that the rest of us don't? How can we do the same thing?

What these people accomplished wasn't luck. But, in a way, it *was* magic– *the powerful magic of Consumer Insight.*

In each case, these marketers knew something important about people. About their customers. About their employees.

They had a unique vision– an insight. Once they knew it, they used it. They used it to invent new products. They used it to design better marketing programs. They used it to build stronger sales plans. And they used it to create some really great advertising as well.They all used Consumer Insight.

This book will teach you some of the skills you'll need to gain those insights. How to enhance your powers of observation. How to watch and listen to people– carefully, deeply and with empathy. And how to learn what they think and how they feel about your brand.

You'll learn to combine those observations and discover the best way to connect your brand with your customer.

Finally, it will give you advice on how to take your insights and inspire people you work with to put together marketing and advertising programs that win in the marketplace.

These three skills comprise the structure of this book. They'll give you the tools you need to solve your own tougher-than-ever marketing problems, by discovering the Consumer Insights critical to your business.

In the first section, you'll read about what we call the Sweet Spot– a special psychological seat of consumer persuasion.

In the second section, we'll cover a variety of tools that help you learn to observe people and their ideas about brands-- not just superficially, but in a way that reveals insights you can effectively use.

In the third section, we'll talk about how to take an insight and use it to inspire; how to organize your observations into meaningful conclusions and communicate them to other people in a way that inspires them to do great work.

Consumer Insight at Work

In the fourth section, you'll have an opportunity to read about how a variety of people put Consumer Insight to work in their daily jobs. You'll hear from people who have developed successful new products and new business concepts, people who have helped inspire great marketing and advertising ideas, and people who have used Consumer Insight in fields as varied as media sales, MIS and brand management.

Finally, in one of the most important features of Section IV, we'll introduce you to the concept of Account Planning, the British-born system for bringing a commitment to Consumer Insight to the advertising agency business. If there's anyone who brings the philosophy of Consumer Insight to life, it's the account planner.

Specifically, you'll learn what account planners do, how they work with other members of the agency team, and how agencies that use account planners make the concept work.

But first, let's talk about you.

13

2 HOW THIS BOOK CAN HELP YOU, WHOEVER YOU ARE

"We have sorted out twenty-two aspects of a true customers-first orientation. Almost all are missing from most management and even marketing texts."

Tom peters

No matter what your job in marketing or advertising, a true insight into your consumers will help you do it better.

If you're a marketing manager, product manager, brand manager or sales manager, a unique insight into your customers will make you a better marketer and advertiser.

Whether you're inventing a new product, designing a package, positioning an old product in a new way, writing a sales strategy or working with your agency, you'll do it better with true Consumer Insight.

You'll learn how to get to know your customers on a level more "personal" than ever before. You'll reach a degree of understanding that will help you build stronger and more enduring relationships with those customers– ones that produce more sales, now and in the future.

If you're an account executive in an advertising agency, this book will help you discover how to think more productively about your client's consumers. Your insights will help you craft better marketing and advertising strategies and help you add value to your relationship with your client.

If you're in the creative arts– a creative director, writer, art director or designer, it will help you learn how to observe people more carefully. You'll open a window onto how they think and feel.

And once you do, you'll see nuances of thought and behavior which inspire your best creative thinking.

If you're already a professional consumer researcher, you'll add new skills for a changing world– how to go beyond the expected for insights that will inspire your colleagues.

If you run an advertising agency, direct marketing firm or public relations firm, this book will help you incorporate a consumer perspective in the way your company works day-to- day. You'll find yourself better able to focus the work of your company's diverse, and sometimes competing, functions on the customers they need to serve.

If you run a small business, you'll learn how to improve the way your business responds to your customer's needs. You'll learn how to manage your employees better as well.

If you're a student, either of the business or in a university, this book will help you understand the foundation on which good marketing has always been built– the consumer. Students who have taken the course on which this book is based have found it helped them internalize the essence of marketing. One student put it this way:

"For the first time, I understand what good marketing means. It doesn't mean telling people about our great product.

It means making our products and our ads <u>act on a Consumer Insight</u>."

It may be tougher than ever to succeed in today's competitive marketplace. But with Consumer Insight, chances are, you'll be one of the winners.

Let's get started.

SECTION I
THE SWEET SPOT

In a mid-season game between the Oakland A's and the Texas Rangers, a promising rookie named Jose Canseco stepped up to the plate. The pitcher, Nolan Ryan, wound up and let his famous fastball go. Canseco swung, connected with a loud crack and blasted the ball right over the centerfield wall.

As Canseco rounded the bases, one of the bat boys picked up the bat he'd dropped, and carried it over to Bert Caulfield, the A's equipment manager. The two of them sat together, heads down, pointing to and talking about a place on the bat.

What were they talking about?

They were talking about one of the things that had made Canseco's hit go so far. They were referring to a special part of the bat– the Sweet Spot.

In sports, the Sweet Spot is that one special place on a baseball bat, golf club or tennis racket that drives the ball farther, faster, and with less effort than when it's hit anywhere else.

Consumers have Sweet Spots too. And when your marketing or advertising idea hits it, your sales will go flying.

Throughout this book, we'll be talking about hitting the Sweet Spot– the place in the consumer's mind where you make a connection between a consumer insight and a brand insight.

You might want to think of it this way:

Consumer Insight + Brand Insight = Sweet Spot

16

3 WHY HITTING THE SWEET SPOT WORKS

*"Above all, the work of an advertising agency
is warmly and immediately human.
It deals with human needs, wants, dreams and hopes."*
Leo Burnett

In 1955, Leo Burnett was looking for a new way to advertise Marlboro cigarettes. One day, the story goes, he saw a *Life* magazine pictorial on cowboys. Something clicked. He instinctively knew that if he could connect Marlboro cigarettes to the idea in that picture, people would respond.

He was right. And, whatever our opinions about the advertising of cigarettes, certainly no one can deny the power of this monumental campaign.

Using the cowboy to represent Marlboro cigarettes was one of the most insightful marketing decisions ever made. That symbol, and the idea it represents, hit a Sweet Spot in all of us– the one that yearns for freedom and independence, for wide open spaces and a far horizon to live out our dreams.

The power of that insight helped make Marlboro the most successful cigarette brand in the country. And, to the extent that people everywhere yearn for the same things we Americans do, it's helped Marlboro become the most successful cigarette in the world.

But we could have lost the Marlboro Man if the Leo Burnett agency and the management of Phillip Morris had not been as intuitively aware of the Sweet Spot as they were.

A number of years later, a respected researcher was hired by Phillip Morris to judge the effectiveness of Burnett's famous Marlboro Man campaign.

His research conclusion: abandon the cowboy. He stated the obvious fact that most Americans weren't cowboys and concluded that they couldn't relate to them as a part of their everyday lives. The techniques the researcher used got at some obvious information (that most people aren't cowboys), but he wasn't able to reach the insight that made the campaign work.

He understood well the facts of the consumer's life, but not the feelings or the fantasies.

Fortunately for Marlboro and Burnett, Phillip Morris management was wise enough to ignore the research.

This story is an important one because it shows that the Sweet Spot isn't always apparent to the naked eye, or detectable by every research tool.

And sometimes the most powerful insights can be well hidden in the obvious.

Another Example

Once upon a time, a little movie connected with its audience so well that it racked up a grand slam home run for its producer, Disney Films.

How many of you saw "Pretty Woman" at least once?

For anyone who knows women, that "surprise" hit should not have been much of a surprise at all. Any woman who saw and loved it could tell you it touched a dream she's always harbored, even if she's a bit embarrassed about it.

'PRETTY WOMAN'

Up on the screen, "Pretty Woman" played out our fantasy. It showed us that, just as we've always hoped, if we're in the right place at the right time, someone rich, handsome, sophisticated and kind will see us for who we really are and carry us off on his white horse. Or his white limousine. And we'll all live happily ever after.

Wouldn't that be nice?

This fantasy, of course, has been around for at least as long as little girls have been raised on Cinderella. Yet, how many other moviemakers have had the insight to tap into that fantasy, particularly in this pragmatic day and age? Or, more important, how many have had the inspiration to execute it so well?

The box office sales of "Pretty Woman" were only exceeded by one other movie in 1990. It was called "Ghost." What Sweet Spot do you imagine it hit? What fantasy did that one exploit?

At this point, you may wonder: if the Sweet Spot is as easy to recognize as all that, why don't marketers hit it all the time?

When we don't connect, it's generally for one of two reasons.
1. We don't dig deep enough to uncover the real insights- into our customers and brands.

2. We have the brand's insight, but don't use it.

Let's look at some examples.

Plymouth & Mitsubishi

The Plymouth Laser and the Mitsubishi Eclipse were identical sports cars. They were both manufactured by a joint venture between Chrysler and Mitsubishi. They offered the same features. They sold for the same price- about $11,000.

Both car companies even targeted the same people: men and especially women, 25-35, well-educated, professional, earning over $40,000 a year.

Doesn't seem much different. But there was, in fact, a considerable difference.

In 1990, Chrysler's 3,000 dealers sold 40,000 Lasers while Mitsubishi's 500 dealers sold 50,000 Eclipses. Amazing! One hundred cars per Mitsubishi dealer, 13 per Chrysler dealer.

What's going on here?

Simple. Mitsubishi knew the target's Sweet Spot and how to hit it. Chrysler didn't.

First of all, Mitsubishi figured with an unknown and foreign name, they should appeal to curious and experimental younger car buyers- people who are willing to try something different, people who want to be different themselves. And, they realized that their car could appeal to women, who now make up a larger than ever percentage of the car market.

So, they geared their marketing and advertising to take advantage of those insights.

They started with the name. The word "eclipse" sounds like an event- like something important happening. It's something likely to appeal to those people who want to see themselves on the leading edge.

Next, Mitsubishi spent 37% of its total advertising budget– $35 million– in the several months before the introduction of the car, so the launch would seem like a big event, too.

Furthermore, they reached out to their target. For example, they sponsored a contest for aerobics instructors to see who could sign up the most people for test drives. The result? 5000 test drive sign-ups.

Their advertising wasn't the run-of-the-mill story of style, horsepower and speed. The ads featured female drivers and an image that the car was the "in" thing to own.

Now let's look at Chrysler. They implemented a traditional auto marketing campaign, aimed largely at men, with ads in car buff magazines, featuring the traditional quality and engineering story.

Eclipse dug for the insight. Laser let it slide.

The Eclipse hit. The Laser missed.

More Marketing Strike-Outs

This kind of thing happens fairly often. In new product development alone, the failure rate is a stunning 90%. The new business failure rate is also quite high– 80% of new business ventures fail in the first five years. Yet, no company invests in a new product and no entrepreneur begins a business expecting failure. Fortunately, if a marketer misses the first time around, sometimes there's a chance to correct the mistake on the rebound.

We're sure Chrysler studied Mitsubishi's great success with the Eclipse and then made appropriate improvements to their own marketing program.

And today we all know that even a marketer as large and successful as Coca-Cola isn't infallible.

"New Coke" was a fascinating example of a marketer misreading its own market. Thinking it could take share from Pepsi by making its taste "consumer-preferred," Coke failed to realize that people drink the history and tradition of a product as much as they do the beverage itself. Upon the introduction of the "New Coke" formula, consumer protest formed, and Pepsi, naturally, used it as an opportunity to trumpet its own successes.

The best laid plans of a very smart marketer were judged to be not so very smart after all when the "facts" of extensive research and taste tests were blown away by the feelings of loyal Coke drinkers.

However, after realizing their mistake, Coke regrouped and recovered very well. The "return" of the now-new "Classic Coke" nearly doubled shelf space overnight. Not a bad mistake to make.

RCA, on the other hand, was not so lucky.

Do you remember videodiscs? In the early 1980's, video-discs were going to be a revolution in home entertainment. And RCA's SelectaVision was destined to be the big winner. Ten years of R&D time and money went into the perfection of the technology. But videodiscs never had a chance. The problem was the VCR.

With a videodisc, people could watch all sorts of movies and shows at home, but with a VCR they could do the same, plus record programs from their TV's. Which would you buy?

Today, however, the story is a little different. With a large base of consumers using VCR's, the videodisc is growing as an adjunct video source because of its superior audio and video characteristics. But the inability to understand the consumer's preference for control of video programming caused RCA to spend millions on a technology out of step with consumer needs, while the competition surged ahead.

The organizers of the USFL also missed their mark. They figured that the football fan, having nothing to watch after the Super Bowl, would leap at the chance to see a different pro league play all spring and summer. They even had opinion research that statistically reaffirmed their judgment.

But, reality has a way of breaking the statistical surface. The habits of all those who said they "might like to watch" football in the spring or summer were just too ingrained to change. To virtually everyone, football meant fall.

The problem was compounded by the needs of two other "consumer" groups– owners and players, each with its own agenda. Bidding wars for a few star players upped the ante. At the same time, lower-than-expected fan interest depressed the pay-off, making it all less worthwhile to the owners and potential advertisers.

The league was wisely abandoned.

The new NFL-sponsored World League of American Football just might find the Sweet Spot, however. By controlling player costs, looking for markets, such as Europe, where minor league football will still be the best game in town, and adding the blessing of the NFL, the new league's story may have a happier ending.

A Few Advertising Strike-Outs

Inspired by the gritty, urban appeal of Levi's 501 button-fly jeans, the very traditional Lee Jean company ran black and white ads on TV and in magazines showing kids in convertibles and at the laundromat wearing Lee Jeans. The ads won awards for creativity, but consumers couldn't make the connection between the images in the ads and their own ideas about Lee.

Reebok's "Let UBU" campaign aimed at individualistic young people. The campaign created an off-the-wall image for the shoes. But even its target thought, "I may want to be me, but do I want to be *that?*" Reebok is now taking a much different tack with their ads.

We could go on– particularly in today's tougher-than-ever market. That's easy. There's a tougher question.

How do you increase the chances of a profitable hit instead of an expensive miss?

First, you learn to think like a consumer.

You have a head start on being a smarter marketer because you already think like a consumer. But sometimes, when you get to work and put on your marketing hat, you forget the world you live in and enter the world you work in.

It's time to get back to what you already know.

4 YOU ALREADY KNOW MORE THAN YOU THINK

"People aren't interested in you.
They're interested in themselves."

Dale Carnegie

The first thing you already know is that every sale, even if it happens via a mass medium, is an individal one. You don't ever buy anything that doesn't fill a want or need you *personally* have. Neither does anyone else.

What did you buy last?

A particular candy bar because it's *your* personal favorite? A pair of shoes because they looked good and felt good on *your* feet? A bottle of perfume because it made *you* feel special? A certain newspaper or magazine because it had a story *you* especially wanted to read?

As Don Schultz of Northwestern University says, "The fifth 'P' of marketing is Personalization." The classic Four P's of Marketing– Product, Price, Place (Distribution), and Promotion– are only effective to the extent that they're used to make a "personal" connection with the consumer.

It bears repeating: ***Every sale is a personal sale.***

Our success as marketers and advertising people comes only when we bring a customer an idea, product or solution that makes things better or easier for him or her *personally.*

To do that, we have to know two things.
1. Who our customers or prospects really are.
2. How they look at life.

Getting To Know All About You

You might think, I already know my target. Adults 25-49, with high school educations or better, living in A and B counties, making $30,000+ each year, and with two or more children in the house between 6 and 18 years of age.

Or, you might say– I even know them better than that. Twenty percent use our brand, 20% are Brand X users and 60% of them are Brand Y users. Or, 70% of them are heavy users, 20% are medium users, and 10% are light users of the category. Or, half of them are brand switchers and half are brand loyalists.

Now, switch gears for a moment and think about yourself. How would you tell somebody else about who you are? Think of two or three things that you think are particularly revealing about you as a person– the couple of things someone would have to know to *really* understand what you're all about. Write them down here.

What Somebody Ought To Know About Me

1.

2.

3.

Now, look them over carefully. If you're like most people, very few of the things that are truly revealing about you have anything to do with either your demographics or your purchasing habits.

If you were going to describe yourself would you say, *"Hi, my name's Mary and I'm a 18-49 -year -old heavy cream cheese user. I'm a brand switcher when it comes to laundry detergent, but loyal to Ragu spaghetti sauce. I have a high school plus education and I'm a frequent fast food user, a superpremium beer drinker, and recently, I've become a catalog shopper. Other than that, there's not much to tell."*

Of course you'd never talk about yourself that way. Yet, all too often, that's exactly how we describe our customers. Consumers become oversimplified groups and bundles of shallow statistics.

Statistics alone do as much good describing people as a ruler does measuring a beach ball. First, it won't wrap all the way around. Second, even if you manage to measure the diameter of a large sphere, it tells you nothing about summer, sand or sunny days. Statistics simply don't encompass the whole picture.

Thinking Like A Regular Person

Even when we know more than the basics about our customers, we still often forget to think about life from their point-of-view.

Once again, thinking about yourself can begin to help you overcome this blind spot.

On your own individual path in life, you look at the world from the vantage point that path gives you.

You think about what's important to you– your job, your house, your kids, your hopes and dreams, your problems and opportunities. None of us thinks very much about anything that isn't relevant or interesting to us– at least not for very long.

But somehow, when we put on our marketing hats, we act as if our customers think about the whole world in terms of our marketing problems. Even though we know better, we often behave as if our customers have little to do but wait for what we have to tell them.

So another key to improving our marketing skills comes from developing the right point-of-view, learning how to see the world through our customer's eyes.

How To Look At The World
Like A Real Person

Take a minute and try another short exercise.

What's on your mind today? What are you thinking about, worrying about or planning?

REAL PERSON EXERCISE #1

Fill in the space below with the five things that come immediately to mind.

What I'm Thinking About Now

1.

2.

3.

4.

5.

Here are some of the things other people list when they do this exercise. Maybe they're a lot like yours.

1. I wish I could lose ten pounds.
2. I've got two reports to finish by tomorrow.
3. I wonder if I'll ever get promoted in this company.
4. I don't feel like doing anything tonight.
5. I'd better get some exercise today.
6. I wish I knew how to get along with my boss better.
7. I wish my kids would listen to me.
8. I'd better get my checking account balanced tonight.
9. I think it's about time to junk this car.
10. What should I have for dinner?

If you look closely at each item on the list, it will be apparent that people don't think about themselves the way we marketers usually talk about them. The most common word is "I."

A person says: "What should I have for dinner?"

A marketer says: "We need to increase the average purchase frequency of Le Menu frozen foods."

A person says: "I don't feel like doing anything tonight."

A marketer says: "We need to communicate the superiority of our chain of movie theaters over video rentals."

A person says: "I think it's about time to junk this car."

A marketer asks: "How might we switch Foreign- Auto-Preferrers to Lincoln-Mercury?"

And we know better. Virtually every marketing class and textbook teaches us first about consumer wants and needs. We're told over and over again: people don't buy 4-inch drill bits; they buy 4-inch holes.

REAL PERSON EXERCISE #2

The next time you begin a marketing or advertising project, or perhaps with the one you're working on right now, ask yourself three questions:

1. Am I defining my customers the way they think about themselves?

2. Am I looking at life from their point-of-view?

3. Am I thinking about ways to bring my products and services to them, rather then expecting them to come to me?

And that's the first giant step toward developing that important *Consumer Insight.*

PRINCIPLE I

Consumer Insight + Brand Insight= Sweet Spot

5 BREAKTHROUGH ADVERTISING

"People look at what interests them, sometimes it's an ad."

Howard Gossage

To this point, we've spoken in general about marketing from the consumer's point-of-view. It's also important to say a few words about advertising from the same perspective.

Advertising clutter is a problem all advertising people are concerned about. According to the _Wall Street Journal_, we're each exposed to 300 ads a day. Some say ten times that. Whatever the number, it's a lot– and growing all the time.

No wonder marketing and advertising people are worried about how well an ad "breaks through the clutter." Everyone knows that you can't persuade someone until you get his or her attention. Or, as the saying goes, "You can't save souls in an empty church."

That makes sense. The only problem with the typical idea of "breakthrough" is the assumption that getting someone's attention is under the *advertiser's* control. Often, we assume that by making an ad faster, brighter, louder, more intrusive or more outrageous, we'll *make* people pay attention, thereby increasing the number of people we ultimately persuade. Somehow we'll jump off the page with our cleverness, or burst through the screen with our technique. And, of course, we'll "ask for the order."

Consequently, there's a general belief that "soft" advertising or "image" advertising doesn't work. Particularly, in today's tough marketplace. It seems that the attitude of most of our advertising is that people must be bludgeoned or bedazzled before they will listen.

This view is reinforced by the fact that many fast, bright, loud, intrusive and outrageous commercials have done very well. Think about Federal Express' "Fast Talker," the bright Levi's "Logo" commercial of the early '70s, or the "Hit the ball as loud as you can" tennis commercial for Nike.

What "Breakthrough" Really Means

The very success of those campaigns confuses the issue. Because, despite which "hard" or "soft" sell commercials have or haven't worked, the truth is that the style of advertising has very little to do with what "breakthrough" really means.

It's only advertising which connects with the consumer that truly breaks through the clutter.

That's because attention and persuasion are under the consumer's control, not the advertiser's.

"Breakthrough" happens not when the advertiser *breaks out of* the multitude of advertising messages, but when the consumer *breaks into* the message because he or she sees something meaningful or relevant.

Each of the commercials we mentioned worked exactly that way. Each broke through the clutter by *connecting* with its audience in a meaningful way– not by being loud, fast, intrusive or outrageous per se.

Federal Express understood how business people feel when they're under deadline pressure. Levi's understood exactly the unique sort of anti-fashion fashion statement its customers wanted to make.

And Nike understood competitive-minded athletes in all sports who saw traditional tennis and genteel "tennis whites" as something not for them.

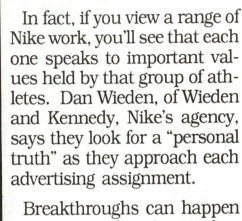

In fact, if you view a range of Nike work, you'll see that each one speaks to important values held by that group of athletes. Dan Wieden, of Wieden and Kennedy, Nike's agency, says they look for a "personal truth" as they approach each advertising assignment.

Breakthroughs can happen as a result of understanding one of those "personal truths," as many great advertising people have intuitively known.

Howard Gossage, the San Francisco ad man quoted at the beginning of this section, made many advertising breakthroughs based on just those kinds of insights.

The *Scientific American* Paper Airplane Contest appealed to exactly the sort of person who would want to read *Scientific American*, whether they entered the contest or not.

His ads for Eagle shirts in _The New Yorker_ set new records for response. They even inspired a book.

His ads for the Sierra Club helped establish the important ecological movement.

He also gave us the Beethoven sweatshirt, and helped introduce us to Marshall McLuhan.

Gossage understood that advertising is "receiver-driven," in the terms of persuasion theorists. What's most important is how it plays on the other side of the page and the other side of the TV screen– how it plays _inside the consumer._

As consumers, we select messages that are relevant and meaningful. And we've become quite good at it, sifting through thousands of messages to find those that interest us.

Think for a moment about the advertising which has been the most meaningful to you. Not the advertising which is simply the funniest or the most entertaining for its own sake, but the advertising which _connects with and speaks to you._

For myself, I think back to the Gallo wine advertising several years ago which showed beautiful, lush vineyards and real people committed to the fine craft of making wine. The commercial was soft; its music was gentle and it hardly said a word. But it connected with the romance of wine and winemaking that I want to believe is true. And, yes, I bought some Gallo wine. _It was fine._

Then there was an old campaign for Lee Jeans. It's a campaign that connected with me. It was a series of ads that truly understood how miserable trying on jeans made me feel. There's nothing worse than going into a store and squeezing yourself into a pair of jeans that's already labeled two sizes bigger than any other pair of pants you own.

Lee understood that and connected with me in their advertising and their products. I believed that Lee Jeans, "The Brand That Fits," could take one of my worst fashion experiences and make it much more pleasant.

As you do the following exercise, you may also find that sometimes the softest advertising speaks the loudest. Because it really doesn't matter how loud or soft the advertising is. What counts is how strongly it resonates with something inside you. Something you already believe or want to believe. Something you want to know more about. Or, something that just plain interests you. Let's look for our own Sweet Spots.

FIND YOUR OWN SWEET SPOT

In the space below, make a list of the advertising messages that *connected* with you recently. For each commercial, try to describe what Sweet spot each hit, and then the real test, indicate if it actually affected your purchase habits. Here's my list.

Product/Ad	Sweet Spot	Purchase Behavior
Lee/"Brand That Fits"	Unpleasant personal experience of trying on jeans in a store	Bought
Gallo/"All The Best"	Matched my feelings of what wine should be all about	Bought

Now for yours.

Product/Ad	Sweet Spot	Purchase Behavior
1.		
2.		
3.		
4.		

As you're doing this, remember that none of us buys everything that appeals to us. I've responded well to ads for Volkswagen, Volvo and Mercedes-Benz, but never owned any of them.

The next time you evaluate an ad and worry about how well it will break through the clutter, ask yourself: how close does it come to the Sweet Spot?

And, if you were a real live person out there in the marketplace, how would you respond? What would make you read yourself into the message?

Those are the real breakthroughs.

PRINCIPLE II
You don't persuade people.
They persuade themselves.

⑥ THE ART OF PERSUASION– USING WHAT YOU ALREADY KNOW

"All life is selling."

Anonymous

Persuading people to do something differently– to buy a new product, to switch to a different brand, or to adopt a new idea– is pretty much how you spend your life as a marketing or advertising person.

But, you spend a great deal of the rest of your life that way too. For example, you persuade your boss to accept your new idea, or your strategy or ad. You persuade your kids to get out of bed in the morning and go to school. You persuade your husband that the Caribbean is a better place for a winter vacation than Colorado.

You do all those things and, in fact, you probably do them very well. So, there's a lot you can apply from your everyday "marketing" successes to the ones you get paid for.

An Example

Here's an exercise I often use to demonstrate just how much you already know. I ask my students to compose a brief letter to their parents, asking for $15,000 to stay in school a year longer than they thought they'd need.

It's interesting how much "consumer" insight is contained in a letter that most people could write in ten minutes or so.

If only the rest of marketing were that straightforward. (Or is it, after all?)

Here's an example of one such letter.

Dear Mom,

I know how much you and Dad have always wanted the best
for me and have tried to provide it. I want you to know
how much I appreciate everything you've done, and I'll
always try to make you proud of what I accomplish in
life.

I especially know that you want me to be successful,
independent and self-supporting. And that's why I'm
writing today. I feel that to get the most out of college
I need to stay here another year. I've learned so much
in the four years I've been here, but there's so much
more to learn. If I could stay another year, I'd take
some classes in marketing, advertising and business
management that would help me use my psychology major
to get a really good job with a good future.

Do you think you and Dad could help me out with one
more year's tuition, room and board? I promise you
it will be a good investment in my future. And do you
think you could help me plan how to talk to Dad about
this?

Thanks Mom. I love you.

If you'll think about this letter the way you think about an
ad or commercial, you'll notice that it is a finely crafted
"marketing" message, designed to connect with a certain
person in a very specific way.

This writer obviously knows her audience very well. She
understands her mother completely and intimately. She
knows what her mother wants for her and knows how a
college degree satisfies it. In other words, she knows her
mother's Sweet Spot and has connected it to the goal she's set
for her letter. Just like real marketing.

Assuming this letter would work, and this student was pretty confident it would, let's look for the "consumer and brand insights" contained in it.

First of all, you'll notice it's written to the student's mother, rather than to both parents or her father alone. And it's clear from the way the letter ends that the writer knows Mom exercises a considerable amount of influence on the important decisions she and Dad make together.

The writer is also aware of what's important to her parents. She knows that they want her to be independent, successful and self-supporting. She also knows they want her to be happy. She tells them that college is making her happy and helping her learn how to accomplish the things that her parents want for her.

In that context, what she wants, "one more year's tuition" (and notice that's how she phrases her request rather than saying straight out she needs $15,000), seems like a good "investment" indeed.

Examining how you go about the same process in your everyday life may just help you discover that marketing is more straightforward than you thought.

Think about people you tried to persuade in just the last day. Write down who you were trying to persuade and what you were trying to accomplish. Remember, you didn't have to be successful to put something on the list. In fact, list at least one attempt that failed. We'll need it later.

PERSUASION ATTEMPTS
People You Tried to Persuade

1.

2.

3.

What You Were Trying to Accomplish

1.

2.

3.

Were You Successful?

1.

2.

3.

As an example, here's one person's list for yesterday.

PERSUASION ATTEMPTS

People I Tried to Persuade

1. My husband

2. Three students

3. A client

4. My client's boss

What I Was Trying to Accomplish

1. Convince my husband we should paint the living room before we renovate the kitchen.

2. Persuade my students to look at their approach to their final project from a different point-of-view.

3. Convince my client that we should redesign the questionnaire for a study we're working on.

4. Persuade my client's boss that we should put off the date for a presentation until the results of a study are re-analyzed.

Was I Successful?

1. Yes

2. Yes

3. Yes

4. No

Not every attempt at persuasion works. But understanding what makes some attempts successful, and other attempts fail will make you a better marketing and advertising person.

Go back to the list you just made and pick out one successful and one unsuccessful attempt at persuasion.

Now, thinking carefully about each, *from the point-of-view of the person you were trying to persuade*, why did one succeed and the other fail? What were the consumer insights you drew on successfully in one attempt? What insights did you fail to see in the other? Write what you've found here.

SUCCESSFUL PERSUASION
What Was The Insight?

How Did You Use It?

UNSUCCESSFUL PERSUASION
What Insight Should You Have Seen?

How Did Your Attempt Miss It?

Here's how the same person analyzed their examples.

SUCCESSFUL PERSUASION
What Was The Insight?
I knew that my husband doesn't really care in what order things are done during our house renovation– just that the house gets back to being somewhat livable.

How Did You Use It?
I showed him we could make more progress by doing something to the living room, which we can't use at all, than by working on the kitchen which is already functional.

UNSUCCESSFUL PERSUASION
What Insight Should You Have Seen?
I should have realized that my client's boss was less concerned with how good the research analysis was than with presenting it on the date he said it would be ready.

How Did Your Attempt Miss It?
I tried to convince him that changing a meeting date was not as bad as presenting bad information. I should have found a way to present something I was comfortable with on the date he'd promised his boss. That way I could have bought myself some time to re-analyze the information I thought wasn't quite good enough.

If your examples are anything like the ones above, you'll see that when you succeeded it was because you knew your "customer" very well. When you failed it was because you didn't have the same degree of understanding.

While it may seem obvious that we need to understand the person we're trying to persuade, ask yourself, how consistently do we really *act* on that fact?

How often, for example, do advertising agencies fail to persuade their clients to produce and run the advertising they've presented? Or that their marketing recommendations should be followed? Or that their fee should be raised?

How often does your boss send you back to do something over again because it wasn't what he or she wanted?

When an idea or proposal doesn't get adopted, it's not always because it just wasn't good enough. More often, the author failed to understand the "client" who needed to buy it.

Unfortunately, sometimes you discover the Consumer Insight only after you've failed. Just like the USFL. Or Coke. You may learn that the client really wanted to accomplish some objective with advertising or marketing other than you thought he did. Or that he tried a campaign somewhat like yours two years ago, failed miserably and looked bad to his bosses. Or perhaps what you've proposed exceeds the budget he planned to spend.

Whatever the reason, the attempt at persuasion failed for the same basic reason the ones in our personal lives fail– because we don't know our customers as well as we should. And, consequently, we can't connect our goals to theirs.

In your personal life, the price of failure is bad enough. In business, the price of failure can be disastrous. You may have to go back and do the ads or the marketing plan over again. The boss or client may get mad at you. After a series of failed attempts, you may even lose your client or be forced to go out of business altogether.

How Not to Persuade People

Recently, _The Wall Street Journal_ ran an interesting article about the consequences of one marketer's lack of insight into the consumers he needed for his business to survive.

Roger Thompson moved from New York to Dallas at the request of his parent company, Barney's, to open a hair salon. He was excited about the opportunity to go because he felt that so many people there were in vital need of the unique product he had to sell.

Mr. Thompson, you see, had a definite opinion about how women's hair should look. He believed in what he calls the "natural look:" short, straight, unbleached and styled without popular gels or sprays.

The women of Dallas, his potential customers, preferred a different style: big, blond and lacquered.

The women of Dallas didn't need Mr. Thompson. They were having their hair done just fine. Mr. Thompson, on the other hand, needed these women desperately. He needed them to accomplish the business objectives he'd been sent to Dallas to achieve. He needed them to survive.

His job was to win them over to a radically different point-of-view. A delicate marketing task at the very least.

What would you do in that situation? How would you embark on the delicate and difficult task he faced?

Mr. Thompson started the ball rolling by _criticizing_ the way his potential clients wore their hair.

He told them their hair was unnatural, unflattering and out-of-date. No one else in the country was wearing her hair that way. To be beautiful and fashionable, he told them, they must adopt his "New York Look."

Guess how these women reacted? How would *you* react? Needless to say, he had a significant lack of customers.

Mr. Thompson violated every principle we talked about earlier. He forgot that every sale is a personal one. And that, when it comes right down to it, no one ever really sells anything at all, *people buy.*

Mr. Thompson might have taken some advice from Bob Middlemas, chief of the new Nordstrom store in Oak Brook, Illinois, a company world-renowned for its unique customer insights:

"It's very well understood in our system that, without customers, there aren't jobs, there aren't opportunities. And the minute we lose sight of that fact, we're just another store selling clothes."

People can always go somewhere else.

Looking at the world through the customer's point-of-view is something good marketers have always known they must do. In the early 1900s, Claude Hopkins, a very successful advertising copywriter said:

"The advertising man studies the consumer. He tries to place himself in the position of the buyer. His success largely depends on doing that to the exclusion of everything else."

Claude Hopkins

Dale Carnegie, author of the famous <u>How to Win Friends and Influence People,</u> opens one chapter of his book by saying, *"I often went fishing up in Maine during the summer. Personally, I am very fond of strawberries and cream, but I have found that, for some strange reason, fish prefer worms.*

So when I went fishing, I didn't think about what I wanted. I thought about what they wanted. I didn't bait the hook with strawberries and cream. Rather I dangled a worm or a grasshopper in front of the fish and said: 'Wouldn't you like to have some of that?'"

Mr. Thompson could have avoided a lot of his problems by being a little more observant of what his fish want to eat. He might have asked himself *why* Dallas women like their hair so blond and big. What purpose does it serve for them? How does it fit with their idea of femininity? Of regional pride? How do they feel about hairstyles imported from New York? How do they feel about changing their hairstyle at all? He could have used the answers to these questions to select his bait.

Now a lot of people might give up Mr. Thompson's goal as hopeless. But I would argue that with a foundation of good consumer insight, and his natural charm, he could have built some measure of success.

He could have changed his *product*– offering hairstyles that appealed to his customer, or he could have changed his *appeal*– developing a more effective way of persuading Texas women to change their hairstyles, and more effective targeting of those who might consider it.

Most of us make mistakes at one time or another, but if we learn from them, that alone can be an *Insight.*

PRINCIPLE III
The first step toward success is putting yourself
in your customer's shoes.

SECTION II
HOW TO FIND
THE SWEET SPOT

"To learn to be a bullfighter,
you must first learn
how to be a bull." Anonymous

As we said, the key to connecting with consumers is being able to put yourself in their shoes.

You need to know how to think the way they think, and feel the way they feel. You have to know what's important to them, what makes them happy, and what they worry about. In other words, you have to learn how to get inside their skin and see the world through their eyes.

It's easy to build the outlines of people's lives with information– when they get up, what they eat for breakfast, the brands of products on their table. But what you're really after is more than an outline. You're after the color and the texture- the *insight* you can use to make your products more appealing and your advertising more persuasive.

We often gather a lot of information about consumers, but seldom insight. It's not easy. Insights are often hard to find.

First, your job will get in your way. Although marketing should mean *acting on a consumer insight*, we generally have very little time for consumers. There are meetings to attend, phone calls to answer, reports to write, presentations to make, commercials to produce. How can you find time to talk to consumers when you barely have time for lunch?

And, sometimes, your own human nature will tend to get in your way. Throughout your marketing or advertising career, you'll be selling to people very much different from yourself.

Sometimes they're older and sometimes younger and many of them may make a lot less money than you. They will not live where you live, eat the way you do or share your taste in movies and music. They may not believe the same things you believe about politics, religion or social mores. They may want completely different things out of life.

We've a tendency to distance ourselves from people unlike ourselves. We maintain that distance both physically and psychologically. When we do come into contact with them, it makes us a little uncomfortable. We sense we don't have a lot in common or that we don't belong.

In many focus groups, the marketing and advertising people are glad there's a one-way mirror separating *us* from *them.* We keep our distance.

Instead of overcoming that gulf, and getting to know people personally and individually, we tend to rely on stereotypes and oversimplifications to think about our target customers.

And it's reflected in our work.

You can readily see this problem when you take a look at a lot of advertising aimed at senior citizens. Advertising people (who tend to be under the age of 40) often see older people as either frail, slow and fearful, or as exactly like 25- year-olds, with exactly the same vocabulary and the same sense of humor. Seldom in-between. And that's how they position the products they advertise. As things that combat the frailty and despair of old age, or as part of a 25- year-old lifestyle that never ends.

Most advertising people don't see the elderly the way they see themselves– as people with great experience of life and maybe even a little wisdom after all those years.Whether it's a result of our jobs or our natures, we can't afford to let this happen.

It undermines our very effectiveness as marketing and advertising people.

So what do we do?

Jumping in Feet First

The secret is to make the time to *immerse* yourself in the people you're marketing to. To live them, breathe with them and study them from every angle.

In that sense, your work is much like that of an actor preparing for a part. You have to "take on" the personality of your consumers the way an actor "takes on" the personality of the character he or she is to play. To be a good bullfighter, become the bull.

Actors who do that well can convince you that they really have *become* someone else. Rent some movies starring Robert DeNiro such as "Raging Bull," "Godfather II," or "Taxi Driver." You'll see someone who immerses himself so well that you believe he really is Jake LaMotta, Vito Corleone, or Travis Bickle, an obsessed cab driver.

Meryl Streep has the same talent and skill. She's completely believable as a Danish baroness in "Out of Africa" and equally believable as Sophie, the Polish concentration camp survivor in "Sophie's Choice."

On the other hand, many other actors are most adept at playing themselves. In every movie she makes, Elizabeth Taylor plays Elizabeth Taylor and in every movie he made, Cary Grant played Cary Grant. They are entertaining to watch, but they don't convince you they're someone else.

All too often, marketers take an approach that worked in one situation and try to make it work in a new one. It's a natural instinct. We all like to repeat our successes. But we're not Cary Grant or Elizabeth Taylor, with roles made to take advantage of what we do well.

We have to prepare for each new part we play in the marketplace.

Immersing yourself in the lives of other people means you have to get out there with them, into the places they live, work, shop and play.

It's a lot of work and it's not for the faint-hearted. But the simple fact is you can't learn enough to connect with your consumers by locking yourself away in your office reading the results of a marketing research study.

For the rest of this section, we're going to explore a variety of tools and techniques that will help you immerse yourself.

As you read about them, keep in mind that no one tool will give you a complete understanding of your customer, or your brand from your customer's point-of-view. But taken together, they can give you a rich consumer experience you'll find meaningful.

But before you head out for your first consumer encounter, you need to tune your antennae.

And the best way to do that is to learn to read yourself.

7 LEARN HOW TO READ YOURSELF

"Being entirely honest with yourself is a good exercise."
Sigmund Freud

That's right, the best place to start is with yourself. This section is about learning how to observe yourself as a consumer. After all, you can't do a really good job of observing and interpreting someone else's behavior, motivations or feelings until you can observe and be honest about your own.

As you develop this skill, you'll gain two valuable benefits.

First, you'll learn how to observe the little things. You'll pay attention to the small, subtle nuances of thought and behavior that can reveal powerful ways to connect with other people. And when you can learn to pay attention to the nuances of your own behavior, you'll pay better attention to the subtleties of other people's behavior.

And, you'll have a starting point for navigating through others' experiences with a product. You'll develop some hypotheses - a "rough outline" to compare and contrast the behaviors, feelings and ideas of others.

An Exercise

The best way to learn it is to do it. Start by picking a product you use. Anything will do. Here's a list of things you might try:

a candy bar

a bar of soap

a bottle of hand lotion

a meal at a fast food place

a cup of coffee

a bottle of furniture polish

a tube of lipstick

a bag of potato chips

a new pair of shoes

some car wax

Now use that product, just as you normally would, but pay attention every second to what you're doing, how you're feeling and what you're thinking as you use it. Notice as much detail as you possibly can.

This is not an easy task. You'll probably have to practice it several times before you get the hang of it. It's hard developing two minds, one to go through the experience itself and another to watch yourself while you do it.

As a first hint, remember, if you're doing it right, it should feel a little awkward. You'll be truly "self-conscious," not in a neurotic way, but in a very observant one.

Let's say you chose a candy bar to practice with, maybe a Snickers. As you pick it up, what do you see? How does it feel in your hand? What does the package make you think? Can you smell anything? Does your mouth anticipate the taste or texture? How? What are you thinking now?

As you open the package, observe. Are you neat or sloppy? Fast or slow? Do you rip it open or peel it back like a banana? How do you hold it in your hand? Can you smell anything now? What do you see right now?

How do you eat it? Do you nibble or bite? Do you force yourself to eat more slowly than you would really like? How does the way you eat it affect your enjoyment of it? When you bite it, how does it feel against your teeth? What does that make you think about?

Do you taste the whole thing or the caramel separate from the chocolate separate from the peanuts? Was the first bite the best? Does the way it tastes change as you come closer to the end? Is it a candy you eat mindlessly, or do you concentrate on it the whole way through?

When are you eating it? How hungry were you? Do you eat a Snickers bar differently than you would another type of candy, say M&Ms? What's the most salient or most memorable part of the experience of eating a Snickers bar?

Now that you've really pigged out, write down some notes on the process while it's still fresh in your mind.

Try to have the notes ready, and if the process can be broken up into "chunks" you might want to make notes at various stages along the way. One thing, however, we haven't yet quite figured out is how to unwrap a candy bar and take notes about it while doing so.

Some people use a tape recorder, and speak into it while they do whatever it is they're studying. Then again, comments you make while actually eating a candy bar may not indeed be all that helpful to the process.

Now think back on the experience. What interesting things did you notice? Was there anything you never thought to pay attention to before? Was there some part of the experience that really captured the feeling of the whole thing?

Sometimes those seemingly small details can lead to some very powerful advertising ideas.

Consider the Oreo™ cookie. What immediately comes to mind? If you're like most, you think about the way " a kid'll eat the middle of an Oreo first... and save the chocolate cookie outside for last!" That tiny detail of experience has been used to create a connection with consumers that has helped reinforce Oreo's position as one of the best (not to mention best-selling) cookies in America.

And it's an *insight* that's been useful for more than just advertising. It inspired the creation of the line extension "Double Stuff." Nabisco truly understands the essence of the consumer's experience with their brand.

Eureka!

Several years ago, the advertising for Eureka vacuum cleaners took advantage of another tiny detail of behavior to create a powerful positioning for the brand.

The next time you vacuum, pay close attention to exactly how you're feeling while you're doing the work. What's the part of vacuuming that makes you feel like you're really accomplishing something?

Is it when you go over a piece of carpet and hear the dirt being sucked in and rattling up the nozzle of the machine? As a lot of people hear the dirt grind and grate, they think to themselves "ha, ha– now I've got you!"

Admittedly, it's a small feeling, a tiny feeling really. No one spends *that* much time pondering the vacuuming experience. But going through the exercise of vacuuming themselves, that's exactly what the creative team noticed.

And when they learned from the Eureka technical center that a carpet can hold *five times* its weight in hidden dirt, they found a Sweet Spot. They connected on insight into the consumer with an insight into the brand.

"Eureka gets the hidden dirt."

In every television commercial, a Eureka owner does battle with the unseen enemy– the dirt lurking in her carpet.

Animated commercials created all sorts of situations for the dirt characters to try to evade the vacuum cleaner. But, like a hungry anteater, the Eureka found the dirt wherever it was hiding– and got it. It's exactly what every person who vacuums wants to feel she's doing too.

EXERCISE

Here are a few more things you can do to practice the techniques of observing yourself (these are harder):

Get ready to go to work
Read a magazine or newspaper
Go to the mall
Decide with someone else about where to go for dinner
Go someplace you've never been before

(You might want to make your own Consumer Detective kit with some note cards, or a note pad and a pen. Perhaps a tape recorder to help keep track of your observations.)

Objectivity vs. Detachment

At this point some of you may be thinking: *Wait a minute. I always thought good consumer behaviorists needed to be objective and scientific. This could hardly be called an exercise in detachment. This can't be science. Where's all the rigor? Where are the big random samples? Aren't I just projecting my own ideas and values onto other people?*

These are, in fact, excellent questions. To answer them, it's important to remember that insightful marketing requires as much sensitive observation as it requires science and valid statistics.

Insights are seldom arrived at objectively. After the fact, we can often find ways to prove our hypothesis in a rigorous manner, but, as Einstein said:

"The supreme task of the physicist is to arrive at those universal elementary laws from which the cosmos can be built

by pure deduction. There is no logical path to these laws; only intuition resting on experience can teach them."

Generally speaking, marketing people are very well trained in the science and statistics part. It's often those other skills that can use some improvement.

Our goal in learning to better read ourselves is, obviously, to become more sensitive to others by learning to observe ourselves as consumers first.

But remember, just reading this chapter and doing an exercise or two doesn't make you an expert at observing yourself. (Not to mention observing others.) It takes considerable, constant practice.

Try repeating the "introspection" exercises we described above at regular intervals. It will help.

As you're doing them, remember to ask yourself:

1. What's the essence of the product experience for me?
2. What subtleties or nuances of my behavior reinforce the product experience?
3. What am I noticing about my own experience with a product that I can use to understand someone else's experiences?

Now that we've practiced our ability to observe ourselves, it's time to learn about our consumers. But from now on, every project you work on, in addition to reading every report and market study, don't forget to take time to read *yourself.*

PRINCIPLE IV

If you want to understand your customers,
the best place to start is by understanding yourself.

8 DATA AND INFORMATION- LAYING THE FOUNDATION

"You gotta know the territory."
The Music Man

As a first step on any project, you have to experience the product to the best of your ability. You have to shop for it, eat it, wear it, drive it and use it. You have to observe yourself.

As you practice the principles we discussed in the previous section, out of the corner of your eye, you may be watching other people doing what you're doing.

But before you start to come to conclusions, you have to *get oriented* to what the market for your product is all about. In case you thought this was all "touchy-feely" subjectivity, *now* is the time for a little objectivity.

You need to understand the facts of a marketplace: how big it is, whether it's been growing, who the competition is, how they're positioning themselves, how successful they are, what trends are affecting the market and, in broad strokes, who the target consumer is, and how they see your brand.

This is where surveys, industry statistics, opinion polls and the like can be helpful. They give you data– the *facts*, things you need to form your own insights. This is your foundation; the solid facts on which your larger insights will rest.

Primary and Secondary Research

As you begin, you should know there are two basic types of research studies you can use: primary and secondary.

Primary research studies are the ones you create to study precisely the topic in which you're interested. An advertising tracking study done by IBM, or a product attitude and usage study done by Procter & Gamble, are examples of primary studies which would answer marketing questions those companies might have.

Primary research studies are also done to measure market sales and share. Nielsen and IRI are two companies which measure sales of products sold in retail outlets. The financial services industry, the fast food industry and the automotive industry each rely on the surveys sponsored by different market research firms to keep track of sales and market share trends.

Often, the company which makes the product you're marketing will have some primary consumer research or marketplace research they will share with you. They may have, for example, sales figures, regional sales differences, seasonality trends in sales, best-selling varieties and awareness figures. These are all bits and pieces of primary research data which can be helpful to you, at least as a starting point.

Secondary research studies are those which have not been commissioned by a single user, and which are made available to a variety of users. The data and information contained in these studies may not answer your specific questions, but they can give you a general understanding of what the market for your product might be.

For many topics, because it's so expensive to conduct primary research ($50,000 for a nationally projectable study is not uncommon), secondary sources are good ones to explore first. For the rest of this chapter, we'll attempt to acquaint you with a variety of "secondary" sources.

If you need or want primary research, there are many first-rate suppliers who can help, and many large marketers have people who specialize in just this important task. It may be vital to your own project at some point to do some primary research. But if you've explored the secondary sources first, you'll be able to spend your primary research money much more wisely.

There are many, many places to find this kind of hard data and information. We'll take a brief tour of five of them just so you know where they are–
      Demographic/product use/media habit surveys
      Public opinion trend studies
      Motivational studies
      Trade magazines and other industry sources
      The federal government

Get the Facts:
Demographics/Product Use/Media Habits

Simmons (SMRB) and Mediamark Research, Inc. (MRI) are two of the largest resources and the ones which most advertising agencies and universities have in- house.

Both of these companies sell large sample demographic/product use/media habits studies. A comprehensive questionnaire is sent to a nationally representative sample of people and they're asked to record products and brands they use, which television shows, magazines and radio stations they choose and what their demographic characteristics are.

MOUTHWASH/DENTAL RINSE: USAGE IN LAST SEVEN DAYS
(ADULTS)

	TOTAL U.S. '000	ALL USERS A '000	B % DOWN	C % ACROSS	D INDX	HEAVY USERS 8 OR MORE A '000	B % DOWN	C % ACROSS	D INDX	MEDIUM USERS 6-7 A '000	B % DOWN	C % ACROSS	D INDX	LIGHT USERS 5 OR LESS A '000	B % DOWN	C % ACROSS	D INDX
TOTAL ADULTS	178193	123932	100.0	69.5	100	29091	100.0	16.3	100	44252	100.0	24.8	100	50589	100.0	28.4	100
MALES	85056	57269	46.2	67.3	97	12168	41.8	14.3	88	21177	47.9	24.9	100	23923	47.3	28.1	99
FEMALES	93136	66663	53.8	71.6	103	16922	58.2	18.2	111	23075	52.1	24.8	100	26666	52.7	28.6	101
18 - 24	25713	17684	14.3	68.8	99	3686	12.7	14.3	88	6442	14.6	25.1	101	7556	14.9	29.4	104
25 - 34	43283	29248	23.6	67.6	97	6362	21.9	14.7	90	10141	22.9	23.4	94	12744	25.2	29.4	104
35 - 44	34804	23918	19.3	68.7	99	5356	18.4	15.4	94	8195	18.5	23.5	95	10366	20.5	29.8	105
45 - 54	23902	16983	13.7	71.1	102	4018	13.8	16.8	103	6212	14.0	26.0	105	6753	13.3	28.3	100
55 - 64	21733	15350	12.4	70.6	102	4369	15.0	20.1	123	5223	11.8	24.0	97	5757	11.4	26.5	93
65 OR OLDER	28796	20749	16.7	72.2	104	5299	18.2	18.4	113	8038	18.2	28.0	113	7413	14.7	25.8	91
18 - 34	68997	46932	37.9	68.0	98	10048	34.5	14.6	89	16583	37.5	24.0	97	20300	40.1	29.4	104
18 - 49	115841	79113	63.8	68.3	98	17245	59.3	14.9	91	27769	62.8	24.0	97	34099	67.4	29.4	104
25 - 54	101990	70149	56.6	68.8	99	15737	54.1	15.4	95	24548	55.5	24.1	97	29864	59.0	29.3	103
35 - 49	46845	32181	26.0	68.7	99	7197	24.7	15.4	94	11186	25.3	23.9	96	13799	27.3	29.5	104
50 OR OLDER	62351	44819	36.2	71.9	103	11846	40.7	19.0	116	16483	37.2	26.4	106	16491	32.6	26.4	93
GRADUATED COLLEGE	32799	20798	16.8	63.4	91	4450	15.3	13.6	83	6871	15.5	20.9	84	9477	18.7	28.9	102
ATTENDED COLLEGE	32672	22534	18.2	69.0	99	5088	17.5	15.6	95	7743	17.5	23.7	95	9704	19.2	29.7	105
GRADUATED HIGH SCHOOL	70684	50238	40.5	71.1	102	11993	41.2	17.0	104	18585	42.0	26.3	106	19661	38.9	27.8	98
DID NOT GRADUATE HIGH SCHOOL	42039	30361	24.5	72.2	104	7560	26.0	18.0	110	11053	25.0	26.3	106	11748	23.2	27.9	98
EMPLOYED MALES	60732	39889	32.2	65.7	94	8280	28.5	13.6	84	14322	32.4	23.6	95	17287	34.2	28.5	100
EMPLOYED FEMALES	49968	34738	28.0	69.5	100	9037	31.1	18.1	111	11788	26.6	23.6	95	13913	27.5	27.8	98
EMPLOYED FULL-TIME	97991	66361	53.5	67.7	97	15387	52.9	15.7	96	23260	52.6	23.7	96	27714	54.8	28.3	100
EMPLOYED PART-TIME	12710	8266	6.7	65.0	94	1930	6.6	15.2	93	2850	6.4	22.4	90	3487	6.9	27.4	97
NOT EMPLOYED	67492	49304	39.8	73.1	105	11774	40.5	17.4	107	18142	41.0	26.9	108	19389	38.3	28.7	101
PROFESSIONAL/MANAGER	29483	19304	15.6	65.5	94	4275	14.7	14.5	89	6514	14.7	22.1	89	8516	16.8	28.9	102
TECH/CLERICAL/SALES	36012	24078	19.4	66.9	96	5798	19.9	16.1	99	8448	19.1	23.5	94	9832	19.4	27.3	96
PRECISION/CRAFT	14266	9476	7.6	66.4	96	2241	7.7	15.7	96	3473	7.8	24.3	98	3761	7.4	26.4	93
OTHER EMPLOYED	30939	21770	17.6	70.4	101	5003	17.2	16.2	99	7675	17.3	24.8	100	9092	18.0	29.4	104
SINGLE	38354	26117	21.1	68.1	98	5747	19.8	15.0	92	9357	21.1	24.4	98	11013	21.8	28.7	101
MARRIED	107815	74998	60.5	69.6	100	17245	59.3	16.0	98	26707	60.4	24.8	100	31047	61.4	28.8	101
DIVORCED/SEPARATED/WIDOWED	32024	22816	18.4	71.2	102	6099	21.0	19.0	117	8188	18.5	25.6	103	8530	16.9	26.6	94
PARENTS	59509	40856	33.0	68.7	99	8669	29.8	14.6	89	13389	30.3	22.5	91	18798	37.2	31.6	111
WHITE	153416	105251	84.9	68.6	99	24348	83.7	15.9	97	37167	84.0	24.2	98	43736	86.5	28.5	100
BLACK	19771	15397	12.4	77.9	112	4070	14.0	20.6	126	5798	13.1	29.3	118	5529	10.9	28.0	99
OTHER	5005	3284	2.6	65.6	94	*672	2.3	13.4	82	1286	2.9	25.7	103	1325	2.6	26.5	93
NORTHEAST-CENSUS	37709	28004	22.6	74.3	107	6641	22.8	17.6	108	11171	25.2	29.6	119	10192	20.1	27.0	95
MIDWEST	43858	28601	23.1	65.2	94	5810	20.0	13.2	81	9113	20.6	20.8	84	13678	27.0	31.2	110
SOUTH	61120	45261	36.5	74.1	106	11849	40.7	19.4	119	15034	34.0	24.6	99	18378	36.3	30.1	106
WEST	35505	22066	17.8	62.1	89	4792	16.5	13.5	83	8933	20.2	25.2	101	8342	16.5	23.5	83
NORTHEAST-MKTG.	39614	29468	23.8	74.4	107	7058	24.3	17.8	109	11469	25.9	29.0	117	10942	21.6	27.6	97
EAST CENTRAL	25102	17361	14.0	69.2	99	3734	12.8	14.9	91	5765	13.0	23.0	92	7862	15.5	31.3	110
WEST CENTRAL	29609	18900	15.3	63.8	92	3635	12.5	12.3	75	6156	13.9	20.8	84	9109	18.0	30.8	108
SOUTH	53267	39125	31.6	73.5	106	10601	36.4	19.9	122	13000	29.4	24.4	98	15524	30.7	29.1	103
PACIFIC	30601	19077	15.4	62.3	90	4062	14.0	13.3	81	7862	17.8	25.7	103	7153	14.1	23.4	82
COUNTY SIZE A	74178	51590	41.6	69.5	100	12001	41.3	16.2	99	19146	43.3	25.8	104	20442	40.4	27.6	97
COUNTY SIZE B	53234	36614	29.5	68.8	99	9236	31.7	17.3	106	12610	28.5	23.7	95	14768	29.2	27.7	98
COUNTY SIZE C	26987	18772	15.1	69.6	100	4286	14.7	15.9	97	6598	14.9	24.4	98	7888	15.6	29.2	103
COUNTY SIZE D	23793	16956	13.7	71.3	102	3568	12.3	15.0	92	5897	13.3	24.8	100	7491	14.8	31.5	111
METRO CENTRAL CITY	54244	37729	30.4	69.6	100	9584	32.9	17.7	108	14254	32.2	26.3	106	13888	27.5	25.6	90
METRO SUBURBAN	82717	56956	46.0	68.9	99	12990	44.7	15.7	96	19611	44.3	23.7	95	24355	48.1	29.4	104
NON METRO	41232	29247	23.6	70.9	102	6517	22.4	15.8	97	10384	23.5	25.2	101	12346	24.4	29.9	105
TOP 5 ADI'S	40038	27699	22.4	69.2	99	5935	20.4	14.8	91	11252	25.4	28.1	113	10512	20.8	26.3	92
TOP 10 ADI'S	56175	39146	31.6	69.7	100	9037	31.1	16.1	99	14706	33.2	26.2	105	15403	30.4	27.4	97
TOP 20 ADI'S	81501	56023	45.2	68.7	99	12927	44.4	15.9	97	20511	46.4	25.2	101	22585	44.6	27.7	98
HSHLD INC. $60,000 OR MORE	19957	13176	10.6	66.0	95	2964	10.2	14.9	91	4630	10.5	23.2	93	5582	11.0	28.0	99
$50,000 OR MORE	31697	21239	17.1	67.0	96	4885	16.8	15.4	94	7304	16.5	23.0	93	9050	17.9	28.6	101
$40,000 OR MORE	53998	36326	29.3	67.3	97	8056	27.7	14.9	91	12913	29.2	23.9	96	15357	30.4	28.4	100
$30,000 OR MORE	83793	57124	46.1	68.2	98	12923	44.4	15.4	94	20210	45.7	24.1	97	23990	47.4	28.6	101
$30,000 - $39,999	29795	20798	16.8	69.8	100	4867	16.7	16.3	100	7297	16.5	24.5	99	8634	17.1	29.0	102
$20,000 - $29,999	34040	24106	19.5	70.8	102	5899	20.3	17.3	106	8552	19.3	25.1	101	9655	19.1	28.4	100
$10,000 - $19,999	38419	26526	21.4	69.0	99	6404	22.0	16.7	102	9666	21.8	25.2	101	10457	20.7	27.2	96
UNDER $10,000	21942	16175	13.1	73.7	106	3865	13.3	17.6	108	5823	13.2	26.5	107	6487	12.8	29.6	104
HOUSEHOLD OF 1 PERSON	22006	15276	12.3	69.4	100	3713	12.8	16.9	103	5999	13.6	27.3	110	5563	11.0	25.3	89
2 PEOPLE	57453	40419	32.6	70.4	101	9912	34.1	17.3	106	14708	33.2	25.6	103	15798	31.2	27.5	97
3 OR 4 PEOPLE	71838	49314	39.8	68.6	99	11384	39.1	15.8	97	16901	38.2	23.5	95	21030	41.6	29.3	103
5 OR MORE PEOPLE	26896	18923	15.3	70.4	101	4081	14.0	15.2	93	6644	15.0	24.7	99	8198	16.2	30.5	107
NO CHILD IN HSHLD	106426	74188	59.9	69.7	100	18291	62.9	17.2	105	27732	62.7	26.1	105	28164	55.7	26.5	93
CHILD(REN) UNDER 2 YRS	14122	9272	7.5	65.7	94	1809	6.2	12.8	78	3160	7.1	22.4	90	4303	8.5	30.5	107
2 - 5 YEARS	26410	17448	14.1	66.1	95	3162	10.9	12.0	73	6117	13.8	23.2	93	8170	16.1	30.9	109
6 - 11 YEARS	33185	23374	18.9	70.4	101	4988	17.1	15.0	92	7758	17.5	23.4	94	10628	21.0	32.0	113
12 - 17 YEARS	33008	23677	19.1	71.7	103	5553	19.1	16.8	103	7659	17.3	23.2	93	10465	20.7	31.7	112
RESIDENCE OWNED	122907	85542	69.0	69.6	100	20189	69.4	16.4	101	30088	68.0	24.5	99	35265	69.7	28.7	101
VALUE: $70,000 OR MORE	60160	41074	33.1	68.3	98	9591	33.0	15.9	98	14671	33.2	24.4	98	16811	33.2	27.9	98
VALUE: UNDER $70,000	62747	44468	35.9	70.9	102	10598	36.4	16.9	103	15417	34.8	24.6	99	18454	36.5	29.4	104

BASE: ADULTS	TOTAL U.S. '000	MICHELOB CLASSIC DARK A '000	B % DOWN	C % ACROSS	D INDEX	MILLER HIGH LIFE GENUINE DRAFT A '000	B % DOWN	C % ACROSS	D INDEX	MILLER HIGH LIFE A '000	B % DOWN	C % ACROSS	D INDEX	MILWAUKEE'S BEST A '000	B % DOWN	C % ACROSS	D INDEX
ALL ADULTS	178281	1990	100.0	1.1	100	8000	100.0	4.5	100	11194	100.0	6.3	100	3199	100.0	1.8	100
MEN	85035	1454	73.1	1.7	153	5500	68.8	6.5	144	7377	65.9	8.7	138	2050	64.1	2.4	134
WOMEN	93246	536	26.9	.6	51	2500	31.3	2.7	60	3817	34.1	4.1	65	1148	35.9	1.2	69
HOUSEHOLD HEADS	101395	1361	68.4	1.3	120	5337	66.7	5.3	117	7031	62.8	6.9	110	2304	72.0	2.3	127
HOMEMAKERS	102573	961	48.3	.9	84	3972	49.7	3.9	86	5239	46.8	5.1	81	1575	49.2	1.5	86
GRADUATED COLLEGE	31271	503	25.3	1.6	144	1846	23.1	5.9	132	2138	19.1	6.8	109	477	14.9	1.5	85
ATTENDED COLLEGE	32228	549	27.6	1.7	153	2124	26.6	6.6	147	2231	19.9	6.9	110	557	17.4	1.7	96
GRADUATED HIGH SCHOOL	69392	789	39.6	1.1	102	2937	36.7	4.2	94	4068	36.3	5.9	93	1114	34.8	1.6	89
DID NOT GRADUATE HIGH SCHOOL	45389	*149	7.5	.3	29	1093	13.7	2.4	54	2758	24.6	6.1	97	1050	32.8	2.3	129
18-24	26460	542	27.2	2.0	184	1836	23.0	6.9	155	2211	19.8	8.4	133	*461	14.4	1.7	97
25-34	43285	735	36.9	1.7	152	2981	37.3	6.9	153	3370	30.1	7.8	124	1004	31.4	2.3	129
35-44	34153	*255	12.8	.7	67	1511	18.9	4.4	99	2093	18.7	6.1	98	528	16.5	1.5	86
45-54	23496	*142	7.1	.6	54	662	8.3	2.8	63	1263	11.3	5.4	86	*458	14.3	1.9	109
55-64	22626	*191	9.6	.8	76	525	6.6	2.3	52	1115	10.0	4.9	78	*381	11.9	1.7	94
65 OR OVER	28262	*124	6.2	.4	39	485	6.1	1.7	38	1143	10.2	4.0	64	*366	11.4	1.3	72
18-34	69744	1277	64.2	1.8	164	4817	60.2	6.9	154	5580	49.8	8.0	127	1465	45.8	2.1	117
18-49	115832	1612	81.0	1.4	125	6654	83.2	5.7	128	8427	75.3	7.3	116	2181	68.2	1.9	105
25-54	100933	1132	56.9	1.1	100	5154	64.4	5.1	114	6726	60.1	6.7	106	1990	62.2	2.0	110
EMPLOYED FULL TIME	101695	1329	66.8	1.3	117	5856	73.2	5.8	128	7364	65.8	7.2	115	1839	57.5	1.8	101
PART-TIME	11602	*63	3.2	.5	49	*530	6.6	4.6	102	620	5.5	5.3	85	*154	4.8	1.3	74
SOLE WAGE EARNER	33693	524	26.3	1.6	139	1917	24.0	5.7	127	2400	21.4	7.1	113	727	22.7	2.2	120
NOT EMPLOYED	64984	598	30.1	.9	82	1614	20.2	2.5	55	3211	28.7	4.9	79	1206	37.7	1.9	103
PROFESSIONAL	15286	*162	8.1	1.1	95	847	10.6	5.5	123	865	7.7	5.7	90	*101	3.2	.7	37
EXECUTIVE/ADMIN./MANAGERIAL	14533	*298	15.0	2.1	184	973	12.2	6.7	149	948	8.5	6.5	104	*261	8.2	1.8	100
CLERICAL/SALES/TECHNICAL	34157	389	19.5	1.1	102	1694	21.2	5.0	111	2216	19.8	6.5	103	*382	11.9	1.1	62
PRECISION/CRAFTS/REPAIR	13836	*115	5.8	.8	74	826	10.3	6.0	133	1256	11.2	9.1	145	*241	7.5	1.7	97
OTHER EMPLOYED	35484	*428	21.5	1.2	108	2046	25.6	5.8	128	2699	24.1	7.6	121	1008	31.5	2.8	158
H/D INCOME $60,000 OR MORE	23842	*333	16.7	1.4	125	1325	16.6	5.6	124	1612	14.4	6.8	108	*266	8.3	1.1	62
$50,000 - 59,999	16373	*124	6.2	.8	68	859	10.7	5.2	117	1001	8.9	6.1	97	*133	4.2	.8	45
$35,000 - 49,999	38392	422	21.2	1.1	98	2366	29.6	6.2	137	2833	25.3	7.4	118	697	21.8	1.8	101
$25,000 - 34,999	31792	399	20.1	1.3	112	1382	17.3	4.3	97	2135	19.1	6.7	107	442	13.8	1.4	77
$15,000 - 24,999	32570	*489	24.6	1.5	135	1365	17.1	4.2	93	2031	18.1	6.2	99	842	26.3	2.6	144
LESS THAN $15,000	35312	*223	11.2	.6	57	704	8.8	2.0	44	1583	14.1	4.5	71	819	25.6	2.3	129
CENSUS REGION: NORTH EAST	38166	*302	15.2	.8	71	1227	15.3	3.2	72	2897	25.9	7.6	121	*132	4.1	.3	19
NORTH CENTRAL	43768	498	25.0	1.1	102	2356	29.5	5.4	120	3682	32.9	8.4	134	930	29.1	2.1	118
SOUTH	60933	650	32.7	1.1	96	2095	26.2	3.4	77	3273	29.2	5.4	86	1637	51.2	2.7	150
WEST	35414	540	27.1	1.5	137	2321	29.0	6.6	146	1342	12.0	3.8	60	*500	15.6	1.4	79
MARKETING REG.: NEW ENGLAND	9686	*130	6.5	1.3	120	363	4.5	3.7	84	1004	9.0	10.4	165	*18	.6	.2	10
MIDDLE ATLANTIC	31069	*195	9.8	.6	56	1076	13.5	3.5	77	2135	19.1	6.9	109	*225	7.0	.7	40
EAST CENTRAL	25139	*272	13.7	1.1	97	1197	15.0	4.8	106	2188	19.5	8.7	139	*500	15.6	2.0	111
WEST CENTRAL	28755	*307	15.4	1.1	96	1465	18.3	5.1	114	2030	18.1	7.1	112	801	25.0	2.8	155
SOUTH EAST	31991	*374	18.8	1.2	105	758	9.5	2.4	53	1627	14.5	5.1	81	863	27.0	2.7	150
SOUTH WEST	20167	*203	10.2	1.0	90	1002	12.5	5.0	111	1057	9.4	5.2	83	480	15.0	2.4	133
PACIFIC	31474	509	25.6	1.6	145	2137	26.7	6.8	151	1153	10.3	3.7	58	*312	9.8	1.0	55
COUNTY SIZE A	75038	888	44.6	1.2	106	4079	51.0	5.4	121	4764	42.6	6.3	101	741	23.2	1.0	55
COUNTY SIZE B	52854	791	39.7	1.5	134	2376	29.7	4.5	100	3655	32.7	6.9	110	1206	37.7	2.3	127
COUNTY SIZE C	26664	*253	12.7	.9	85	965	12.1	3.6	81	1751	15.6	6.6	105	*619	19.3	2.3	129
COUNTY SIZE D	23725	*57	2.9	.2	22	*579	7.2	2.4	54	1025	9.2	4.3	69	*633	19.8	2.7	149
MSA CENTRAL CITY	63360	863	43.4	1.4	122	3201	40.0	5.1	113	4679	41.8	7.4	118	1237	38.7	2.0	109
MSA SUBURBAN	73656	839	42.2	1.1	102	3620	45.3	4.9	110	4526	40.4	6.1	98	953	29.8	1.3	72
NON-MSA	41265	*288	14.5	.7	63	1179	14.7	2.9	64	1989	17.8	4.8	77	1009	31.5	2.4	136
SINGLE	37775	859	43.2	2.3	204	2728	34.1	7.2	161	3255	29.1	8.6	137	822	25.7	2.2	121
MARRIED	108540	876	44.0	.8	72	4014	50.2	3.7	82	6082	54.3	5.6	89	1845	57.7	1.7	95
OTHER	31965	*255	12.8	.8	71	1259	15.7	3.9	88	1858	16.6	5.8	93	531	16.6	1.7	93
PARENTS	60645	402	20.2	.7	59	2605	32.6	4.3	96	3948	35.3	6.5	104	1087	34.0	1.8	100
WORKING PARENTS	45672	325	16.3	.7	64	2288	28.6	5.0	112	3263	29.1	7.1	114	846	26.4	1.9	103
SOLE PARENT	9134	*60	3.0	.7	59	409	5.1	4.5	100	621	5.5	6.8	108	*222	6.9	2.4	135
HOUSEHOLD SIZE: 1 PERSON	21914	*302	15.2	1.4	123	859	10.7	3.9	87	1117	10.0	5.1	81	*258	8.1	1.2	66
2 PERSONS	55277	640	32.2	1.2	104	2238	28.0	4.0	90	3164	28.3	5.7	91	999	31.2	1.8	101
3 OR MORE	101090	1048	52.7	1.0	93	4903	61.3	4.9	108	6914	61.8	6.8	109	1942	60.7	1.9	107
ANY CHILD IN HOUSEHOLD	73418	615	30.9	.8	75	3194	39.9	4.4	97	4784	42.7	6.5	104	1459	45.6	2.0	111
UNDER 2 YEARS	14139	*121	6.1	.9	77	718	9.0	5.1	113	823	7.4	5.8	93	*387	12.1	2.7	153
2-5 YEARS	25587	*171	8.6	.7	60	1330	16.6	5.2	116	1919	17.1	7.5	119	564	17.6	2.2	123
6-11 YEARS	33017	*251	12.6	.8	68	1482	18.5	4.5	100	2079	18.6	6.3	100	650	20.3	2.0	110
12-17 YEARS	33793	*257	12.9	.8	68	1158	14.5	3.4	76	2031	18.1	6.0	96	508	15.9	1.5	84
WHITE	154028	1637	82.3	1.1	95	6956	87.0	4.5	101	9175	82.0	6.0	95	2505	78.3	1.6	91
BLACK	19599	*273	13.7	1.4	125	889	11.1	4.5	101	1827	16.3	9.3	148	623	19.5	3.2	177
SPANISH SPEAKING	10301	*138	6.9	1.3	120	521	6.5	5.1	113	692	6.2	6.7	107	*153	4.8	1.5	83
HOME OWNED	121083	1189	59.7	1.0	88	5057	63.2	4.2	93	7057	63.0	5.8	93	2006	62.7	1.7	92

Spring 1989

MRI differs from Simmons in that it incorporates how much of a product consumers use (volume) and not just whether they use it at all (penetration). Volume helps you understand how important "heavy" users are to your product category. For instance, it's a rule of thumb in many categories that 20% of the users consume 80% of the volume.

The results of the studies are printed in a series of bound books in which you can look up information, but many companies also have the databases on-line, which means that you can configure the data anyway you like to answer specific questions you might have.

For example, if you're marketing or advertising a brand of beer, let's say Old Style (a regional beer with sales concentrated in the Midwest), before you start developing marketing plans and writing ads, you would be interested in the basic demographic facts about the men who drink that beer compared to the people who drink other brands of beer. Simmons and MRI will tell you that.

The "Index" numbers compare the demographics of "male Old Style drinkers" to those of "total men." Any time the index is over 100, the Old Style drinkers are more likely to have this characteristic than are men in general. When the index is less than 100, they're less likely.

Here's some information from MRI.

Male Old Style Drinkers
(index versus Total Men)

Age	%	Index
18-24	13	85
25-34	28	111
35-44	21	103
45-54	14	101
55-64	14	116

Occupation

Prof/Manag	22	112
Cler-Sales/Tech	16	105
Prec/Crafts	16	109
Other	28	110

Income

$40,000+	53	130
$30-40,000	21	125
$20-30,000	14	80
under $20,000	12	48

You realize looking at this bit of information that Old Style drinkers are men of all ages and all professions. Income skews a little higher than average, tending to be over $30,000.

A pretty broad group of people. But it's a start.

You also know, if you've examined your own beer drinking habits (assuming you're a beer drinker) that you probably don't drink just one brand of beer. You might have a favorite, but there are others you'll accept if the bar is out of your brand. You might buy a variety, depending on what's on special. Let's imagine other people are like you. Assume the database is on- line. Let's reconfigure the MRI data that way.

Male Old Style Drinkers
(index versus Total Men)

Old Style Most Often			Old Style Sometimes	
Age	%	Index	%	Index
18-24	5	35	20	138
25-34	22	87	34	136
35-44	17	83	25	123
45-54	23	165	5	34
55-64	18	148	10	83
Occupation				
Prof/Manag	19	100	24	124
Cler-Sales/Tech	12	80	19	130
Prec/Crafts	16	109	16	110
Other	28	113	27	107
Income				
$40,000+	48	118	58	143
$30-40,000	16	92	27	160
$20-30,000	18	99	11	59
under $20,000	19	77	4	2

This analysis reveals a more interesting picture indeed. It shows that the "core" Old Style drinker, the person who drinks the brand most often, is considerably older than the man who drinks it only occasionally. Besides being younger, the occasional drinker also tends to be "white collar" and is likely to have a higher income.

If you add to that the fact that the majority of beer consumption comes from men under the age of 35, you get a sense of this brand's marketing problem. Its loyal drinkers are getting older and their beer consumption is declining. And young drinkers aren't drinking Old Style to the same extent they are other brands.

You've just laid down the beginnings of a foundation for revitalizing the brand. You may or may not accomplish it, but you understand the job much more clearly.

Public Opinion Surveys

Other sources of information help you understand your target's general attitudes and opinions.

Roper, Yankelovich and Gallup are three nationally known firms which conduct large-scale attitude surveys on a variety of topics. For example, if you're studying baby food, these sources might be able to tell you something about how today's mothers are different from mothers 10 or 15 years ago. Or, again, if you're interested in beer, they'll show you what's on the minds of young people today.

Roper and Yankelovich each also sponsor a broad public opinion survey which tracks broad trends in the culture-attitudes toward work, family, marriage, religion, etc. to which companies can subscribe– The Roper Report and The Yankelovich Monitor. Some of the major findings from the studies will be published in magazines like *American Demographics* or in books like Daniel Yankelovich's *New Rules— Finding Self-Fulfillment In A World Turned Upside Down.*

66

Here's an excerpt from "The Public Pulse" from The Roper Organization.

SELF-IMPOSED PROHIBITION OF ALCOHOL

"The consumer trend toward 'light' drinks—vodka instead of bourbon, light beer instead of regular beer—points to a more far-reaching trend: a further decline in the number of alcohol users and an ultimate decline in overall consumption.

New, heightened emphasis on health and fitness is likely to endure. This acts to the detriment of products widely perceived rightly or wrongly as unhealthy, particularly cigarettes and alcoholic beverages.

The analogy with cigarettes is significant. Smokers first moved to 'light' low-tar cigarettes—before an ultimate consumption decline set in. Further, smoking became a social issue, not strictly a personal one, as demonstrated by the growth of no-smoking areas in public places.

The same is happening now with alcohol—especially its move into the social terrain via campaigns against drunk driving. Intensifying social pressures on drinkers could lead large numbers of them to abandon alcoholic products."

This could give you something to think about if you were working with a brewery and attempting to give them some help planning new products. For instance, you might look at who's drinking more light beer or trying non-alcoholic beers.

Motivational Studies and VALS

Other companies specialize in studies which can help you understand your target's underlying motivations.

Values and Lifestyles, also known as VALS, is published by SRI International and is probably the best known. The VALS study classifies Americans into nine motivational segments based on Maslow's Hierarchy of Needs, and explains product and brand use in terms of each type's values and lifestyles.

The nine VALS groups are:

Survivors: People in this group are generally economically, educationally and socially disadvantaged. Life for them is a struggle against poverty and hopelessness. Survivors are often fatalistic, superstitious and tend to trust in luck to see them through.

Sustainers: People in this group are slightly better off economically than Survivors, but are still very poor. They tend to be more hopeful in their outlook, however, even though life is a day-to-day struggle.

Belongers: This is the largest VALS group and is close to the stereotype of "Middle America." People in this group are conforming, conventional, traditional and conservative. Home and family are focal in their lives.

Emulators: These tend to be younger, upwardly mobile, status conscious people ("Yuppies," "Puppies," etc.).They're ambitious and competitive and like to "show-off" the things they buy. Pop fads and fashions often start with this group.

Achievers: These are well-to-do people who are well-educated and enjoy the material things life has to offer. They are often leaders in politics and/or business, and are oriented to success, achievement and fame.

I-Am-Me: This groups tends to be young and fiercely individualistic. This is often a stage many young people go through during their student years as they experiment with an expanded variety of life's experiences.

Experiential: These are people who believe that "life is a journey, not a destination" and they want to experience life to its fullest. They are active and participate in a wide variety of sports, hobbies, crafts and activities.

Societally Conscious: This group tends to focus on social responsibility as the core of their lives.They believe in simplicity, conservation, frugality and inner growth. They tend to be very well-educated and intellectual in orientation.

Integrated: These are people who have achieved a high degree of psychological maturity. They tend to be tolerant and take a broad, long-term perspective on life. They're also self-expressive and aesthetically aware.

Products are often positioned at different motivational segments. Working again with our beer example, you can think about how Budweiser might be aimed at Belongers, Heineken at Emulators, imported brands at Achievers and locally produced "microbrews" at Experientials.

Beyond VALS, there are a variety of motivational and lifestyle studies you may find useful. Some are very broad, like VALS, and are meant to explain the attitudes and behaviors of people in general. PRIZM is another example of a study like VALS, but it's based on the idea that the neighborhood you live in reveals the important things about how you see yourself and who you aspire to be.

Consequently, it's a good way to understand your motivations and to predict the kinds of products and brands you might buy. (Cars, for instance. Did you ever notice how everyone in a neighborhood seems to own one of just a few makes of cars?) You can imagine how useful a study like this one might be to someone who markets products that are visible to your neighbors (like lawn mowers) or to someone in the direct marketing business..

But you'll also encounter other kinds of motivational studies that are designed to explain behavior in a variety of particular product categories. For example, there are ones in the financial services category that can be used to help position banking and securities products. You'll find others designed for the fast food industry, the retailing industry, the catalog industry and the travel industry.

You'll also see ones that are created to explain why people buy coffee, or disinfectants or mattresses. Typically, the trade organizations we'll talk about in the next section will have sponsored and paid for studies in their particular category of interest. Members of these organizations have access to these studies. So, often, do people looking for general information. Sometimes they're published in trade magazines or general research magazines like "American Demographics."

Before we go on, it's important to inject a word of caution about all of the various studies you'll encounter in this chapter, but particularly about these motivational and lifestyle studies. They're very appealing, and very tempting. When you first encounter one about the product or category you're studying, you'll think, "Wonderful! Someone else has figured this problem out for me!" *Wrong.*

These kinds of studies are often good thought starters. They're good background information to help you get smart fast. They're also good ways to check ideas and hypotheses you've invented using other techniques. But they're rarely the be-all and end-all of any particular marketing problem. That's because, while they're very generally useful, they're almost never specifically relevant. They may help you understand the motivations for the refrigerated cookie dough category, for instance, but they won't help you solve your specific problem on Pillsbury Slice 'N Bake at the particular moment in time.

It's beyond the scope of this book to go into all of the details of these very interesting studies, or to teach you how to analyze all the information available. But you'll find the addresses and phone numbers of these organizations at the end of the chapter. You can call or write for more information.

The best advice about all this secondary resarch is: find it, read it, absorb it, use it– but never stop there.

Trade and Industry Sources

Consumer and trade magazines can also be excellent sources of secondary information. Many publications have research departments that collect information on their subscriber base, or on the industry they serve. The results of those studies are generally also made available to marketers and their advertising agencies.

In addition, reading these magazines can give you interesting insights on the industry itself. What's on their minds? What's the competition doing? What are the promotional and trade programs that have been successful? What legislative issues might be affecting the industry?

Reading a brewing industry journal won't necessarily help us sell Old Style to our target beer drinkers. But it will add to our better understanding of the particular marketplace in which that brand competes.

Many industries also have trade associations designed to serve the common interests of all the companies in that industry. Some of them are very well known– the American Medical Association, the American Dairy Association, the Prune Board, for example. Others are more obscure. But almost all of them keep track of industry data that can be helpful when you're trying to map out a market. The *Encyclopedia of Associations* is a reference guide to what thousands of associations do and how to get in touch with them.

Associations and trade journals can give you a perspective on an industry you'd never find anyplace else.

The Federal Government

Finally, don't underestimate the usefulness of information collected by the federal government. Sometimes, the bureaucratic waters are difficult to navigate, but virtually every agency of the government collects facts and statistics about various aspects of the American population. You can get particularly good information about trends they measure over time. Most of this information is available free of charge, though it often takes a while to get.

The *United States Government Manual* and the *Statistical Abstract of the United States, 1990* are good sourcebooks for the types of information the government has, and are both available at the reference desks of most libraries.

The Census Bureau can be particularly helpful. The branch of the bureau called User Services can tell you where to find the information you're looking for and how to order it, or they can refer you to the proper branch within the bureau. The phone number is listed at the end of the chapter.

Searching Out The Facts Yourself

On-line databases are becoming more common and more inexpensive all the time. Many companies and universities subscribe to one called Lexis/Nexis which allows you to search a wide variety of newspapers, business periodicals and general interest publications yourself. The system is easy to learn and the results are immediate.

Another way to find what's out there is through an information clearinghouse. FIND/svp is one such company. If you subscribe to FIND/svp, it will search every available database and give you information about whatever topic you're interested in. It can be expensive, but using a service like this one can save you hours and hours of searching for information by yourself.

Here is a helpful, albeit incomplete, list of some secondary sources of information. Remember, many of these companies depend on the fees they charge subscribers to fund their research. But it's also true that many of them are sometimes willing to share research that's a few years old. So if you're doing a student project, maybe you can peek at some expensive research from just a few years ago. All you have to do is find the right person to ask.

If you're at a company working to become more consumer-driven, one of your first steps might be to prepare a summary of what secondary source material is available in your category. This list of sources can be a good start.

A base of facts about a given market won't get you all the way to the Sweet Spot, but it can help you gain insights by giving you a more complete knowledge of the marketplace that you need to be most effective.

PRINCIPLE V

Get the facts. When you're exploring a new marketplace, make sure your insights are grounded on facts.

SECONDARY RESEARCH SOURCES

Ameriscope
10 S. Riverside Plaza
Suite 662
Chicago, IL 60606
(312) 258-0050

Claritas
201 N. Union Street
Alexandria, VA 22314
(703) 683-8300
Includes PRIZM.

Data Users Services Division
There is a branch called Customer Services.
(301) 763-4100
They have data for the entire bureau, and can tell you where
to find data, how to order it and can refer you to the proper
branch.

DYG, Inc.
55 Taxter Road
Elmsford, NY 10523
(914) 347-7200
(212) 247-1313

Encyclopedia of Associations
25th Edition
Gale Research, Inc., Publisher
Lists trade associations, what they do and their phone
numbers.

FIND/svp
625 Avenue of the Americas, 2nd Floor
New York, NY 10011-2002
(212) 645-4500

Gallup & Robinson, Inc.
575 Ewing Street
Princeton, NJ 08540
(609) 924-3400
Includes syndicated studies.

Information Resources, Inc.
150 N. Clinton Street
Chicago, IL 60661
(312) 726-1221

Mead Data Center
200 Park Avenue
New York, NY 10166
(212) 309-8100

A. C. Nielsen Company
Nielsen Plaza
Northbrook, IL 60062
(708) 498-6300

The Roper Organization
205 E. 42nd Street
New York, NY 10017
(212) 599-0700

SRI International
333 Ravenswood Avenue
Menlo Park, CA 94025
(415) 326-6200
For VALS information, same company and address.
(415) 859-3882

Simmons Market Research Bureau
380 Madison Avenue, 5th Floor
New York, NY 10017
(212) 916-8900

Statistical Abstract of the United States 1990*
U. S. Department of Commerce
Bureau of the Census

United States Bureau of the Census
(301) 763-5002

United States Government Manual*
Office of the Federal Register, National Archives & Records
Administration.
Lists government agencies and what they do.

Yankelovich Clancy Shulman
8 Wright Street
Westport, CT 06880
(203) 227-2700
Includes the Yankelovich Monitor.
*These books are for sale by Superintendent of Documents, U.S. Government Printing Office, Washington, DC 20402, (202) 783-3238.

9 THE CHALLENGE-FROM DATA TO INSPIRATION

"The shrewd guess, the fertile hypothesis,
the courageous leap to a tentative conclusion.
These are the most valuable coin of the thinker at work."
                                        Jerome Butler

So, we've built a good base of facts, or at least a start. But there's much more to do.

We need to go beyond the basic statistics about our business and our consumer. We need Insights– unique combinations of information that give meaning to the marketplace. And even more than that, we need to inspire the others on our team to create products, marketing ideas and ads that connect with those insights.

That's an important truth about marketing and advertising- we can't do it alone. They're complex activities that involve a lot of people working together. It's a team sport. Data and information aren't enough. We also need more; we need insight and inspiration.

DATA—>INFORMATION—>INSIGHT—>*INSPIRATION*

This is the process at the core of our book. It's a fascinating dynamic. You're simultaneously condensing and expanding your understanding of consumers, and their behavior, as you go along.

You're condensing a lot of information into a single driving insight and you're simultaneously expanding from lots of little pieces of information into one idea that's very big indeed.

Let's take a look now at the process:

77

DATA. It's the first thing we gather. It's the raw stuff which we analyze and convert to information. It is the basis for describing the marketplace, the target consumers and their behavior. When we count who, what, when, where and how, we are generating data. This is the sort of information we obtain from the Census Bureau, from Gallup or from NFO. From primary and secondary sources.

DATA—>INFORMATION. When that data is analyzed, simplified and reported, it becomes information. We spoke of how to get data and information in the last section of this book. This is the foundation which informs our insights. This information is a "map" of the marketplace.

For instance, after analyzing data, we might know how much of our cereal people eat, compared to how much of our competitor's cereal they eat. We might know how people rate our airline on various dimensions of service quality. Or we might know what they consider to be the main selling idea of a commercial they've just viewed.

Charts, tables, graphs, conceptual models or any of a wide variety of tools help us draw a simplified picture of a large complex mass of data.

All too often, this is the point where many researchers and marketers have been trained to stop–when we've turned data into information. Certainly we have a good description, but, by itself, we don't have any real understanding of our consumers.We have not found that critical insight we need for our message to be effective. To get to that elusive point, we have to leap higher and dig deeper. All at the same time.

INFORMATION—>INSIGHT. This is not an easy jump. We're moving from statistical fact into the world of hypothesis. From clean facts to subtle implications. From the security of quantifiable data to the insecurity of qualitative intuition and judgment.

Moving from information to insight requires some creative interpretation. It calls for recognizing patterns in the myriad dots of information that yield up a more complete picture and a deeper understanding of your consumer base. And it also forces you to *question..*

You must take what you know from your base of information and ask questions . Why are people the way they are? Why do they feel the way they do? What are they likely to do next? Where is that spot in their hearts or in their minds (or both) where I need to aim my marketing message?

Remember, the obvious facts are already known to everyone, including the competition. Our very survival as marketers depends on seeing things more deeply or more simply or more clearly than our competitors.

Sometimes what we see is subtle and sometimes it's so obvious we're slightly amazed that no one seemed to notice it before. Good insights often have a simplicity and a clarity that seems obvious after the fact, as marketing pros, Trout & Ries, state in their classic "Positioning" book.

But, just as the obvious facts are known to everyone, so are the obvious insights. Yet, in a world that's changing with the speed of light, there may be a big fresh insight just ready to be discovered. You never know.

Finally, the insights must be *actionable* for our brand. They must be something we can do something about.

INSIGHT—>**INSIGHT—>INSPIRATION.** Ultimately, even insights aren't enough. Insights all by themselves don't inspire people to invent products, strategies or ads that connect.

Insights have to be made to inspire people to act on them. That's the inspiration part. And it's *critical.*

They have to be communicated in such a way that the people who will use them can feel them for themselves. If you can't do that, even with the wonderful insights you may uncover, your work may not be used at all.

This was one of the important contributions of the British Account Planning System. The person who developed the consumer insight was charged with the task of inspiring the creative team to work with it. Account Planners made communicating these insights an integrated part of the complex process of creating advertising, and, as a result, made inspiration part of their job function.

DATA—>INFORMATION—>INSIGHT—>*INSPIRATION*=
JELL-O ™

Here's an example of the process at work. In the late 1970s, market data indicated to General Foods that, in general, consumers were interested in lighter desserts and were less likely to make or buy heavy ones. In response, Young & Rubicam and GF took advantage of Jell-O's unique characteristics (it certainly doesn't *look* heavy) and positioned it as a light, tasty dessert that wouldn't fill you up.

Even though this positioning was exactly what the information told the brand management to do, sales of this 50 year-old brand continued to decline.

More analysis revealed the insight that only one consumer segment was beginning to worry about the lightness or heaviness of desserts. Another segment, much larger, and Jell-O's core consumer, was very committed to dessert, any dessert, as an integral part of a meal.

To these women, more traditional wives and mothers, dessert was the "fun" part of the meal, something you looked forward to while you ate the rest of your dinner.

It's not hard to understand how this insight inspired an enjoyable, effective commercial.

Jell-O, of course, has some very unique properties that

make it an especially fun dessert to have on the dinner table. It wiggles. It jiggles. It bounces around on your spoon. These brand insights merged into an advertising idea, communicated with a memorable song, and topped off with the equally memorable theme line "Make Jell-O gelatin, and make some fun." It hit the Sweet Spot and helped stop the decline of the brand- which had been sliding for some time.

But the brand still wasn't growing.

The "Make Some Fun" advertising helped women to think about Jell-O in the right context, but there was another barrier to using Jell-O that was lurking far below the surface. *It was a "problem" women didn't even know they had.*

As much as they agreed that Jell-O was inherently colorful and fun, these women assumed that the only way to make Jell-O was to pour it in a big mold, let it sit for several hours, and turn it out. Which made them think they had to *plan* to make Jell-O...much farther in advance than they thought was convenient. Other alternatives seemed easier to them.

But the researchers didn't stop there. They did some more probing and found out one more interesting thing. Women didn't really know many interesting ways to make Jell-O.

But...*they didn't know they didn't know.*

With that insight came the inspiration for a new vision of the job of Jell-O advertising: to help women realize that Jell-O was not only fun and rewarding to eat, but easy, versatile and fun to make. The advertising used real women making real recipes, all of which were surprisingly easy and creative. It gave women a lot of new ideas and the confidence to try them.

And they did. Jell-O sales responded immediately.

But insights don't just help you change your advertising. They can also help you change your *product*. Today's mother has more options. And Jell-O has changed with the market.

Today, the "brand equity" for Jell-O has been extended to new products such as Jell-O Pudding and Pudding Pops.

What this example shows is how important it is to keep pushing for the insight. With the right insight, even "old hat" advertising techniques such as recipe advertising can inspire a "breakthrough."

Insight into the consumer and the brand is a much harder job than just cataloging the facts. It requires a real creativity and a great skill at observing and interpreting people.

We'll spend the remainder of this book talking about the value of insight and inspiration.

We'll discuss some techniques for uncovering insights into how consumers think and behave. We'll give you a few more exercises to build your skills. And then we'll focus on the process for making those insights inspirational.

PRINCIPLE VI
DATA->INFORMATION->INSIGHT->*INSPIRATION*

First, we'll see what we can learn from the great detectives of the world.

10 HOW TO BE A REALLY GOOD CONSUMER DETECTIVE

"Elementary, my dear Watson"
Sherlock Holmes

Now we're ready to make the leap from information to insight. So, get yourself prepared for the task. The exercises and examples in this section will help you become more skillful at uncovering these insights.

Watch First, Ask Questions Later

When we try to understand why people do what they do, we usually ask them questions. The consumer research you're probably most familiar with are the ones in which people were directly asked a lot of questions about themselves in surveys, focus groups and in-depth interviews.

Before you try to be a good questioner, it helps to be a good watcher and listener. One of the best ways to get comfortable with watching and listening is to put yourself in situations where you never have to ask a question at all. If you can get good at this, when you actually do ask a consumer a question, chances are it will be a much more productive one.

There's a lot you can learn about this skill from professional detectives. Because, as any good detective will tell you, people may not volunteer everything, but evidence doesn't lie. Learn to read and interpret the evidence present all around you. Then you can almost guess in advance what a person will say.

Spend an afternoon with a good detective and watch what he does. If you can't find a real detective, a fictional one will do. Pick any of the movies on this list and view them. You'll have fun, and at the same time you'll learn to pay attention to the little clues that reveal a lot.

Here's the list of detective movies for your review:

"Chinatown"
"The Thin Man"
"The Maltese Falcon"
"The Day of the Jackal"
"Presumed Innocent"
"The Jagged Edge"
"Body Heat"
"Klute"

Of course the most famous person to do this kind of work was Sherlock Holmes, Sir Arthur Conan Doyle's "consulting detective." Holmes knew how to watch people and what to watch for. He could make incredible deductions from the simplest of observations.

Here's an example of an interchange between Holmes and Dr. Watson in *"The Sign of Four"* in which Holmes demonstrates his skill. Watson has asked Holmes to deduce the character of a man after an examination of his pocket watch.

"There are hardly any data," Holmes remarked. "The watch has been recently cleaned, which robs me of my most suggestive facts."

"In my heart I accused my companion of putting forward a most lame and impotent excuse to cover his failure. What data could he expect from an uncleaned watch?"

"Though unsatisfactory, my research has not been entirely barren," he observed staring up at the ceiling with dreamy, lack-lustre eyes. "Subject to your correction, the watch belonged to your elder brother, who inherited it from your father."

"That you gather, no doubt, from the H.W. upon the back?"

"Quite so. The W. suggests your own name. The date of the watch is nearly fifty years back, and the initials are as old as the watch; so it was made for the last generation.

Jewelry usually descends to the eldest son, and he is most likely to have the same name as the father. Your father has, if I remember right, been dead many years. It has, therefore, been in the hands of your eldest brother."

"Right, so far," said I. "Anything else?"

"He was a man of untidy habits—very untidy and careless. He was left with good prospects, but he threw away his chances, lived for some time in poverty with occasional short intervals of prosperity, and finally, taking to drink, he died. That is all I can gather."

"How in the name of all that is wonderful did you get these facts? They are absolutely correct in every particular."

"Ah, that is good luck. I could only say what was the balance of probability. I did not at all expect to be so accurate."

"But it was not mere guesswork?"

"No, no: I never guess. It is a shocking habit- destructive to the logical faculty. What seems strange to you is only so because you do not follow my train of thought or observe the small facts upon which large inferences may depend. For example,I began by stating that your brother was careless. When you observe the lower part of that watch-case you notice that it is not only dented in two places, but it is cut and marked all over from the habit of keeping other hard objects, such as coins or keys, in the same pocket. Surely it is no great feat to assume that a man who treats a fifty-guinea watch so cavalierly must be a careless man. Neither is it a very far-fetched inference that a man who inherits one article of such value is pretty well provided for in other respects."

I nodded to show that I followed his reasoning.

"It is very customary for pawn brokers in England, when they take a watch, to scratch the numbers of the ticket with a pin-point upon the inside of the case. It is more handy than a

label as there is no risk of the number being lost or transposed. There are no less than four such numbers visible to my lens on the inside of this case. Inference—that your brother was often at low water. Secondary inference— that he had occasional bursts of prosperity, or he could not have redeemed the pledge. Finally, I ask you to look at the inner plate, which contains the keyhole. Look at the thousands of scratches all round the hole-marks where the key has slipped. What sober man's key could have scored those grooves? But you will never see a drunkard's watch without them. He winds it at night, and he leaves these traces of his unsteady hand. Where is the mystery in all this?"

Holmes' ability to observe and interpret the mere physical facts of a person's existence was extraordinary... and also a work of fiction. But, the power of such skills need not be limited necessarily to fiction.

In the somewhat less violent world of the modern market-place, detective work is equally important. What a person wears, how he talks, the kind of car he drives, his brand of beer say volumes about that person's habits and values.

Great insights are often revealed in the little things.

Since defining people by their product habits gives a distorted view, we need to use our detective's magnifying glass.

Detective-in-Training

Being a good detective begins with training yourself to watch for the little things that tell a lot. Once again, you probably know more than you realize.

For instance, if you've ever travelled abroad, how can you tell which people are the Americans? If you've tried a new recipe, how do you know whether people like it without asking them? How can you tell when two people are in love?

Here's another exercise to help you practice.

Below are pictures of three people. In the space provided, write a short description of who you imagine each one is and what you think each would be like. When you're finished, go back and pick out all the little clues that you used (probably unconsciously) to come to your conclusions.

1   **2**   **3**

1.<u>Description</u>   <u>The Clues</u>

2.<u>Description</u>   <u>The Clues</u>

3.<u>Description</u>   <u>The Clues</u>

The little clues people leave about themselves can show you how to connect with them. As we mentioned in the first section, the more you know about your consumers, the better you can make your brand intersect their paths, rather than making them walk over to yours.

Quite literally, for example, a major university waited to put in sidewalks until the students had a chance to walk to classes for a quarter. They put the sidewalks in where the students wore paths in the ground.

A nationally known children's museum found out which were the most popular exhibits by looking at which ones had the most fingerprints on them and which of the hands-on exhibits wore out the fastest. They were able to reorganize the exhibits to attract attention and prevent logjams.

A major cellular phone company used a list of people with vanity license plates as the basis for a direct marketing campaign. They figured that anyone with a vanity plate was pretty involved with his or her car and would probably be a good candidate for a cellular phone.

Irma Zandl, a well-known market researcher who specializes in teens, spends hours in shopping malls, hair salons, record stores, and goes to concerts all over the country just to watch how teens dress, what they do and how they buy. Spending time like this helped her spot teen trends such as Lycra® bike shorts, rap music and tie-dye shirts, long before they hit the swirling teen mainstream.

A small advertising agency with a very "artful" style of advertising realized that the clients who most appreciated their work also tended to have corporate fine art collections at their headquarters. An appreciation for fine art in general indicated, perhaps, a greater willingness to appreciate the "artistic" qualities of that agency's style of advertising. So, the agency used "ownership of a corporate art collection" as one of the ways they qualified new business prospects.

Here are some more ways to practice this skill.

•Get on public transportation and try to deduce what the person you're sitting next to does for a living.

•Go to a restaurant you've never visited before and see if you can discern the sort of patrons it's trying to attract.

•Go to a mall and figure out what it is about a store that makes its customers feel comfortable there. Can you find any stores that seem to be turning their customers off?

•Go to someone's house and deduce what their interests are and what their lifestyle is like. You can do the same exercise in your client's office.

•Look at yourself. What would someone be able to figure out about you by seeing how you dress, walking through your house, going through your closets?

Now, when you're trying to understand your consumers, ask yourself, what clues are these people giving me about who they are? What do those clues mean?

Using "Professional Detectives"

Watching carefully for the clues is something every good insight person does. But to get good insights, you can also use people who spend their lives watching the clues. We call them "professional consumer detectives."

Here's what we mean.

Recently, a small advertising agency was pitching a company that makes men's dress shoes. They had very little time and very little money to get to know the target and decide precisely how to position the shoes.

So they brought in a select group of "professionals" to help them better understand the market. They interviewed professional shoe shine men. It turned out to be a most valuable exercise for them.

No one knows more about shoes and the people who wear them than the men who shine those shoes for a living. They live and breathe shoes. They know which shoes hold together and which fall apart. They can describe the "personality" of every shoe ever made. And they can tell a "Florsheim" man from a "Cole-Haan" man from a "Bally" man at fifty feet. In fact, some of them make a game of guessing and seeing how often they are right.

The clever agency used what they learned as the basis for a presentation including both a strategic and a creative recommendation (and some fancy footwork).

Surprise. The agency won the account.

Virtually every category of products and services has its "professionals." In the beer business, bartenders are worth their weight in gold. Bartenders have a daily opportunity to observe people at their most uninhibited. Some of them could qualify as psychologists. (And, in fact, that's just what some of them fancy themselves.)

Even if he's not quite at that level, a good bartender can tell you all about who drinks which brands, how much, how fast and why. Some of them can also predict which brand a person will order as soon as he walks in the door. They watch for all of the tiny physical signs and clues that expose a person's values and lifestyle. And because a brand of beer so often reflects those very things, a bartender who is also a good observer is often right.

Another Exercise

For each one of the categories below, here are some of the "professional detectives." Can you think of any others? Think about the person who can offer you deeper insights that come from observing large numbers of people that you're intimately interested in.

Category	Detective
Golfers	caddies
Brides-to-be	ministers
Corporate executives	secretaries
Affluent women	manicurists
Chicagoans	taxi drivers

Think about your own consumers. Who spends their time serving them, working with them and watching them? Talk to the "professionals" and see what you can learn.

Using "professional detectives" and learning to be a good one yourself helps to raise your "consumer sensitivity." It follows that chances are better you'll see more deeply and insightfully into people's behavior.

PRINCIPLE VII
Little clues often reveal big insights.

11 ETHNOGRAPHY-LEARNING TO WATCH OTHERS

" When in Rome, do as the Romans do."

Proverb

Now that you have your consumer antennae better attuned, let's try to use them in a more complex situation.

In this section, you'll learn how to observe a person actually using your own product or service. It's a technique called *"ethnography,"* and it's borrowed from the scientific field of anthropology. The dictionary defines "ethnography" as a branch of anthropology dealing with the description of cultures. In a way, that's how you can learn to think about your customers– as an isolated little culture.

What You Can Learn From Margaret Mead

Ethnography is what Margaret Mead practiced with the Samoans. It's what Diane Fossey did with the mountain gorillas. And, way back in 1835, it's what Alexis de Tocqueville did to produce his classic volume, *Democracy in America.*

Ethnography gives you an opportunity to observe, first-hand, what life is like from someone else's point-of-view. It's a little like being a foreign exchange student and living for a while with a family in a culture different from your own.

We're not advocating that you move in with one of your consumers (although it wouldn't be a bad idea and some research firms have done just that). But there are ways of "living" with them, other than moving in. It's an important technique to practice because, as we said, marketing and ad people don't usually live the kinds of lives their consumers do. One agency stays in close touch with Middle America by having their employees regularly spend time in a small town.

93

In some respects, ethnography can be simple and easy. You just have to spend a day doing what your consumers would do. On a Sunday morning, if they go to church, then go. If afterwards, they eat breakfast at the local diner, then do that too. If they come home every evening and watch World Championship Wrestling, then go to the mat yourself. If they have kids and you don't, then borrow one or more for a day (usually quite long enough)!

You get the idea. It seems like obvious advice, but some marketing and advertising people don't even do that much.

Watching People In Action

You can learn even more if you actually watch someone using your product. It can help even more to get what you see on videotape, so you can watch it more than once.

For example, last Thanksgiving, I shot a videotape of my sister bathing her two children, both of whom are under the age of three. In my Consumer Insight class, we show that videotape and the students discuss what they see.

From this particular videotape, the students gained a lot of important insights. They noticed that bathtime is more than just an exercise in getting clean. It's also an opportunity for teaching; about water, soap, ducks, balls and sailboats, and how to bathe a little sister. It's an opportunity for self-expression; for splashing, kicking and dunking. It's an opportunity for mothering and nurturing; for gently washing the child's hair, for patting him dry in a big, soft towel, and smoothing on powder or lotion.

Just from watching a short videotape, it was easy for the students to put themselves in the place of that mother and her children. They went through the experience from another point-of-view. And they remembered bathtime when they were kids, or when they'd bathed nieces and nephews.

Afterward, when I asked them to take what they'd seen and

invent some new bath product ideas and some ways to position current ones, it was amazing how easy the exercise was. The students came up with many, many new product ideas and with a whole variety of ways to position them.

Watching mothers and kids in action was a rich source of insight, and clearly more thought-provoking than just listening to mothers describe bath time in a sterile interview or focus group. It helps to get your feet wet, as it were.

This "hands-on" technique can be time-consuming, but the payoff can be more than worthwhile.

For years, watching children play has helped toymakers design toys children truly like to play with. Watching a person wash dishes could help you invent a new dishwashing detergent or reposition an old one.

Pick one or two of the activities on this list and observe someone engaged in that activity. Get it on videotape if you can. Otherwise, take some good notes.

> Watch a woman put on her makeup.
> Watch a man shave.
> Watch a child fix herself something to eat.
> Watch someone clean the house.
> Watch a person walk a dog.
> Watch someone feed a baby.
> Watch a boy play a computer game.

What do you notice? What ideas for products or positionings does it give you? What's the insight on which you could build a marketing idea or advertising campaign that connects?

Going All The Way

If you take this ethnography idea one step further, you'll find yourself at your consumer's house, spending an afternoon or evening with her and her family, learning about how your product fits into the context of their lives.

We suggest you do just that.

It could be one of the most enlightening experiences you'll ever have. You'll gain consumer and brand insights that may inspire some great marketing and advertising ideas.

Chi-Chi's– When You Feel A Little Mexican

A few years ago, an advertising agency tried this exercise to help them come up with an advertising campaign for a chain of mid-priced Mexican restaurants called Chi-Chi's.

The research people at Young & Rubicam/Chicago recruited several families who ate at Chi-Chi's and asked if they'd let a research person take them out to dinner.

Before dinner, the researcher picked them up at their homes, to see how they lived and to learn a little more about them as people. They spent a little time there discussing how the families liked to spend their time and how they decided where to go out to dinner. The families were even asked to take the researchers on a tour of their homes and point out some favorite rooms and possessions.

Then the researchers took them to the restaurant, sat down, and had dinner with them. They watched how the customers looked at the menu, how they decided what to order, how they ate and what kind of experience they had. They were asked to make comments regarding the food, the service and even the decor.

The agency came away with some valuable insights.

They learned that, for its target, going to Chi-Chi's was akin to being transported to Mexico. Since most of these people would prefer never to venture beyond the limits of an American border, going to Chi-Chi's was an adventure that simulated the real thing.

The food was part of the adventure too. It was totally unlike what they usually ate at home or at any other restaurant. Where else could you have such a wide variety of taste sensations all at one meal? Hot, cold, spicy, creamy, chunky, salty, crunchy and crispy one right after another? And what other restaurant starts the meal with a whole basket of what might as well be Doritos?

For these people, a meal at Chi-Chi's was a meal of total abandon and complete indulgence. It was a meal you half ate with your hands and one where you didn't really start having fun until you spilled something on yourself.

Insights about consumers and about the brand inspired advertising that helped stop a four year sales decline.

Hunter Fans- Built To Last A Lifetime

Another example of an ethnography study that inspired some great advertising was one done for Hunter ceiling fans— the oldest ceiling fan company in America.

In this case, the agency researchers went to the homes of people who owned Hunters and sat in the room where the fan hung and asked them to talk about it.

The stories these people told about their fans revealed what a strong emotional connection they had with them. For some, it was the first piece of furniture a woman and her husband had bought as a young married couple. Others recalled how watching the fan go 'round and 'round kept a small child quiet and contented for hours. Still others spoke with gratitude about the fan that helped relax them during a long, hot and restless night.

For all these people, their Hunter ceiling fan wasn't an appliance. It was a beloved piece of furniture that happened to hang from the ceiling.

The writer and art director, seeing these findings, were inspired to create advertising which tied Hunter's lifetime guarantee to the emotions their owners felt.

An Important Point

Let's just take a moment here to reinforce something in this Hunter advertising that is at the heart of the most effective and persuasive communication- **linking a Consumer Insight with a Brand Insight**. When you can do that, chances are you've hit the Sweet Spot dead center.

Truth is both emotional and rational. In case after case, the richest level of communication comes from combining a rational brand benefit with an emotional need.

It's our little formula again: Consumer Insight + Brand Insight= Sweet Spot.

Again, that's why you have to know your customers as living, breathing human beings. It helps you put the facts of your brand into a valid and meaningful emotional context.

More Good Advice

Spend some time with consumers in the setting in which they feel most comfortable. If you're selling women's clothes, take them shopping and ask them to show you their closets. If you're marketing products through a catalog, ask them to show you what they've bought from your catalog and ask them what they think of it as they go through it with you page-by-page.

If you're selling auto parts or tools, stand with someone while he works on a car, or fixes a faucet, or builds a set of shelves. Chances are, you'll learn a lot about the mechanics of consumers- how they act and react.

And here's an idea to help your professional colleagues move with you from information to insight and all the way to inspiration. Take some photographs, and have slides made. And use them to share any insights you've learned with the rest of your team back at the office.

This is also a good time to mention that general activities

which help you keep up on what's going on with your target are mandatory. Ask your media department what your market's favorite TV shows are. Watch them. Learn which magazines they like and read them. Maybe you wouldn't choose to see "Bill and Ted's Excellent Adventure," but if your target audience would, then you'd better go, Dude.

You have to get inside your target's life and see things from their point-of-view. Make yourself an inquiring student in their "country." Or at least an alert and curious tourist.

You'll find you've learned more than you ever would by just observing, from behind the one-way mirror, a heavily directed focus group session. You may also find, perhaps to your surprise, you've spent time with some very nice people.

And, along the way, you've learned "ethnography."

PRINCIPLE VIII

You'll know consumers better in their natural setting.

12 HOW TO ASK PEOPLE QUESTIONS (AND THEN LISTEN TO WHAT THEY SAY)

"Inquiring minds want to know."
National Enquirer

To this point, we've avoided the subject of how to ask consumers questions in an interview, in favor of encouraging you to practice some other very important but less frequently used skills, like consumer observation and ethnography. Now it's time to talk about questioning techniques. But before we start, there is something important you should keep in mind.

It's easy to ask questions. A two-year-old could do it (and often does).

But asking questions that reveal insights can be a bit tougher. Even more difficult is learning how to listen to what people say and what they don't.

Listening and learning to "read between the lines" is so important because people can't always tell you directly what you want to know. When people recall their behavior, they may not be able to accurately describe what they felt or thought at the time. Or, they may not be able to put what they're thinking into words. They may not want to tell you-especially if you're asking about a sensitive subject.

Finally, they may not even know themselves.

Also, people often say what they think you want to hear. It's a very human thing to gauge our audience and adjust our answers accordingly. There are many research studies that

101

demonstrate how the tone, manner, sex and/or wardrobe of the questioner can have an effect on responses.

Consequently, gaining a unique insight into our consumers depends as much on being a good listener and observer as it does on being a good or clever questioner.

The most important requirement for being a good listener is a true curiosity about what people have to say. Too often we ask consumers what they think only when we're trying to prove an idea we're already committed to. Maybe we want evidence that some marketing strategy is right. Or we want to prove that some ad campaign we're invested in will work.

In that case, we're not really looking for insights, we're looking for confirmation. And, when people sense that's all we're interested in, we get very shallow answers. Marketers and advertising people are led down blind alleys all the time when they ask consumers to tell them that their pre-determined destination is a good place to go.

In today's marketplace, which is far more competitive than ever, we have to learn to be more honest and open-minded. And we have to learn to look a little deeper, past the obvious answers our competition probably knows as well as we do, to the insights that will help us make our products stand apart.

How to Begin

Let's start with how to talk to consumers face-to-face. Once you've mastered this technique you'll find it much easier to question people in groups or to write questions for a survey.

It's also the best place to start, because it is an exercise that shows you how one person thinks and feels. Sitting across a table and looking directly into someone's eyes forces you to pay close attention and concentrate on what they're saying.

102

The first question that marketing and advertising people usually ask is, "Where do I find people to talk to?" It's not that hard. Every city in the country has marketing research firms who will "recruit" consumers to your specifications for a fee. They often randomly call people on the telephone, asking them a variety of product usage and demographic questions to qualify them, and then if they do, the marketing research firm will invite the consumer to participate in an interview. To increase the chances that someone will agree, the firm usually offers them an "incentive" of at least $25.

But what if you don't have much money? This is often the case, especially with a student project. Under those circumstances, it doesn't hurt to use your network of friends, friends of friends and family, at least to start. If you can find people who use the product you're interested in, or are good prospects, then you can begin by interviewing them. Of course if these people aren't representative of the target you're trying to reach, then you have to look for other people who are. Let your good judgment be your guide.

People also ask, "how many people do I need to interview to get the information I want?" "How long should all this take?" Those are harder questions to give a general answer to, but the best rule of thumb is to keep interviewing people until you find the underlying insights about the product or people you're studying. Keep going until you start hearing people tell you the same things over and over, and until your curiosity is satisfied. In some cases this can take as few as 10 or 15 interviews. In other cases, it will require many more, particularly if your target has many subsegments.

How to Have a Good Interview

Now for the interview itself. The whole thing will go very smoothly if you keep one important thing in mind–*the "star" of the interview is the consumer, not you.* While it may seem an obvious point, it's an easy one to forget.

The job is an important one, you're in control and it's a real temptation to "run" the interview. Finding the right conversational flow and tempo is hard– you want the customer to do the leading, yet you're the interviewer.

Here are some important things to keep in mind.

First and foremost, you want to keep the interview as comfortable for the consumer as you can. Many people, particularly if they've never been interviewed before, find the whole situation a little intimidating. You can help put a person at ease if you treat them as a guest rather than as a "subject." It's important because the more the consumer can relate to you, the more you'll learn from the interview.

Here are some other "tricks of the trade."

1. Dress the way your consumer is dressed. Clothes say a lot about a person and you want to make sure yours say the right things. You want yours to say, "I'm like you and we're going to have a good conversation." Dress professionally, but in a way your guest can relate to. You'll get very little out of a conversation with a man who's just finished working at his factory job, if you're sitting there in a $500 suit.

2. Don't take notes if you can possibly avoid it. A tape recorder can be awkward at first, but you and your consumer will soon forget about it and get on with the conversation. Note- taking can make your consumer wonder what it was she said that was important enough to write down, and distracts your attention, placing extra strain on both parties.

3. Tell your consumer why he's there. Marketing and advertising people often think that telling the consumer about the project you're working on somehow biases his answers. If you keep your explanation general and simple, it won't hurt. You don't have to say, "We're having a big argument at the agency about which of two campaigns to recommend. We're showing them to some consumers to settle the fight." You can say, "We're working on some potato chip advertising and we'd like to know more about what people who like potato chips think, so that we can communicate in the best way possible."

4. Tell her you have no vested interest in her answers. Remember that the questioning method people are most familiar with is a test. They know there are right and wrong answers. Many people think that consumer interviews are tests too. Assure them that you're simply interested in what they have to say and why. Let them know that you have no investment in their answers either way. If you do that, a person will feel much more comfortable about telling you what she thinks and how she feels.

5. Act interested in what he has to say. Many people think that unless they sit there with a blank expression on their faces, they'll bias the interview or "lead the witness." Don't worry, you won't. Of course you don't want to overdo it. You don't need to say, "I agree with you completely, that's just what I've been telling the client for weeks," but you can be conversational without going too far.

6. Make the first questions easy to answer. Easy questions like, "Where do you live?" "Where do you work?" "When did you start using Brand X?" help put a consumer at ease. Then if you have more personal or sensitive questions to ask later on, she'll be more comfortable answering them. Also, this gives her time to forget the tape recorder is on.

7. Move from the general to the specific. You always want to put the opinions people have about brands and advertising in the broadest context possible. If you're interested in getting someone's reactions to a new campaign for a brand of frozen dinners, then start out asking what mealtimes are like at the person's home. How often do they eat out as opposed to cooking at home? Under what circumstances are they most likely to fix a frozen dinner? From there, you can move on to more specific questions about your brand, the competition and the advertising.

8. The most important question you can ask is "why." In-depth interviews and focus groups are not small sample replacements for a quantitative study designed to measure how many and how much. Instead, they're a valuable tool for understanding *why* people do what they do. So ask a person "why." If a woman tells you she thinks it's perfectly fine to serve her children a sweetened cereal in the morning, ask why. If, on the other hand, she tells you she never gives her kids sugar in the morning, again ask why. Keep on asking why until you understand why. That's the only reason for the interview in the first place.

9. Watch someone who interviews people for a living. Bill Moyers and David Frost are two good examples. Dick Cavett and Jay Leno aren't bad either. See what you can learn from the way they ask questions and structure their interviews. You can often use what you see to make yourself better.

Obviously, this is very general advice. It's impossible to give you a set of specific questions that will serve you in all circumstances. Instead, what you need is a lot of practice. And, the best place to practice is at parties full of strangers. Talk to them, ask them about themselves, keep them talking until you feel you have an insight about them. Not only will you hone your skills, you'll be the most popular person there. People love to talk about themselves.

How to Listen and Take Notes

Here are a few thoughts to help you really listen to what people say and take better notes as you interview.

1. Listen during your interview as you would during a normal conversation. Focus on your general impressions. Ask yourself, "What are the main ideas I'm getting out of this conversation?" When the interview is concluded, write those impressions down on a notepad.

2. After you've done five or six interviews or a focus group or two, go back and listen to the audio tape. What other things do you notice beyond your first impressions? Are there specific remarks that people made that you think are particularly expressive or insightful?

3. Try to listen to *how* people express themselves as much as to what they say. Let's suppose you're conducting interviews with women who use a particular brand of laundry detergent. You start the conversation by asking what they do during the day. One woman may say, "Well, I'm just a house-wife." Another may say, "I'm a domestic engineer." A third may say, "I take care of two children and work as hard as anyone who works in an office downtown." All three have told you they are homemakers, but each has also revealed an insight into how she feels about it. In addition to her words, a person's body language can also reveal how she feels about what she's saying.

4. Listen for what people *don't* say, too. A married man who tells you that his favorite time to drink beer is in a bar with his buddies may tell you something about how he sees the difference between his "social" and his "family" life.

5. Try to listen for patterns across interviews. What is one person saying that has also been expressed by someone else, perhaps in a different way? What themes keep coming up over and over again?

6. Try not to take everything a consumer says too literally. When talking about products such as automobiles and financial services, people will often describe themselves as totally rational human beings and deny that emotion plays any role in the purchase process. We have yet to see any purchase that is totally rational. So sometimes it's necessary to take what people tell you with a grain of salt.

7. Don't filter what people say through pre-conceived ideas of what the marketing or advertising strategy should be. Try to approach every interview with a fresh and open mind. If someone tells you that service in your fast food restaurant has really declined, resist the temptation to say to yourself, "People always complain about service. What do they expect with minimum wage workers anyway?"

Think about the important insights people are really giving you about their expectations from your restaurant.

How to Ask Questions

Now let's discuss asking questions. There are three standard types of questioning techniques that are especially useful for revealing valuable insights.

1. **Projective Questioning**
2. **Brand Personality**
3. **Laddering**

These methods can help you find additional ways for people to talk about an area that may seem dried up. After you talk about breakfast and making bacon and eating bacon, it can seem like there's not a lot more to say. But there's still a great deal more to learn. And these techniques can help.

Projective questioning helps you gain insights into a person, independent of product use. Brand personality helps you explore purely emotional connections people make with brands. Laddering shows how people connect brand facts to how the brand meets their own needs.

Projective Questioning

Sometimes you can learn the most about your consumers by not really asking them about the product you're marketing at all. This is particularly true when you're working on a product with a strong image component such as beer, cigarettes, perfume, cars or clothing.

In this case, finding out how they think of themselves, and what they aspire to may be more useful for positioning a brand than knowing how they use it.

Here are some examples of "projective" questions.

1. Thinking back on your life so far, is there anything you'd go back and do differently?

2. If you could give a piece of advice to a son or daughter, what would that advice be?

3. What would you like to be remembered for after you're gone?

4. If you could change places with anyone for a day, who would it be and why?

5. If you could go forward or backward in time, which way would you go, where would you go? Why?

6. If money were no object and you could go anywhere in the world for a vacation, where would you go?

7. If you won the lottery tomorrow, how would it change your life?

8. Before you die, is there anything really special you want to do?

9. Have you ever seen a movie that could have been made about you? Is there any movie that really captured how you feel about life?

It's surprising how easily most people answer questions like these and how much they enjoy talking about them.

Questions like these reveal insights, not in terms of a product need per se, but in terms of a consumer's life.

Ask some of your friends questions like these and then think: how would you position a brand of beer to them? A cigarette? A shaving lotion?

Look at some ads for products of the same type: Virginia Slims, Old Spice, Budweiser. What do those marketers know about their customers?

Next, we'll talk about a technique which can help reveal insights into how people think about brands.

Product and Brand Personality

If ketchup were a person, what would he or she be like? If you died and came back as a catalog, which one would it be?

As silly as these questions sound, they're some of the most valuable ones you can ask as you're pushing for an insight. The answers reveal an intangible aura that surrounds every product and brand. We call this aura *personality*. Other people call it *brand image* or, sometimes, *brand equity*.

Products have personalities, just like people. Knowing the personality of a brand can help you understand its strengths, or hidden weaknesses. It can tell you if the brand is an up-and-comer, or is getting a little passe.

You can also think of it as an insight into the *brand*, like the insight you're looking for in your consumers. Connect the two and, bang, you've found a Sweet Spot.

Furthermore, people often use brands with personality characteristics like their own or ones they aspire to possess. Consequently, knowing just the personality of a product can tell you a lot about its users.

Other people take what they've learned about a brand's personality and create a character to bring it to life. There's no one better at that than the Leo Burnett Company. From the Keebler Elves to the Jolly Green Giant to the Pillsbury Doughboy, not to mention the Marlboro Man. Burnett has helped build some of the most enduring brands in America through their insight into a brand's personality and what they call "inherent drama."

AN EXERCISE

Pick any three brands from the list below and quickly, right off the top of your head, list five personality characteristics you associate with each.

Old Spice	Maybelline
IBM	Xerox
Colgate toothpaste	Stouffer's frozen entrees
Tropicana	Barbasol
Maytag	Ruffles potato chips

Brand 1 _____ Brand 2_____ Brand 3_____

1.	1.	1.
2.	2.	2.
3.	3.	3.
4.	4.	4.
5.	5.	5.

Here are some of the things you might have listed.

Brand 1: <u>Tropicana</u> Brand 2: <u>IBM</u>   Brand 3: <u>Maybelline</u>

1. Sunny	1. Strong	1. Pretty
2. Fresh-scrubbed	2. Masculine	2. Unsophisticated
3. Cheerful	3. Arrogant	3. Childlike
4. Energetic	4. Powerful	4. Cute
5. Outgoing	5. Intelligent	5. Whimsical

If you take this exercise a little further, and list the personality characteristics of the major competitor for each brand, you can begin to see how you might take advantage of your brand's strengths or compensate for its weaknesses in advertising and merchandising.

For example, in positioning itself against IBM, Apple Computer was able to contrast itself with the "Big Brother" personality people associated with IBM to communicate a very powerful message in a commercial called "1984."

Maybelline's agency created a campaign called "Smart. Beautiful. Maybelline." to help overcome its somewhat unsophisticated brand personality.

Tropicana, a mainstay of the orange juice industry, introduced a new product called Tropicana Twister and gave it a wacky, off-beat image to add a very contemporary facet to its traditional, wholesome personality.

MORE EXERCISE

Another way to get at the whole issue of brand personality is to ask people to make collages. We often find that people have a much easier time dealing with a concept like "personality" visually, rather than verbally. Asking them to make a collage of pictures cut from magazines gives your consumer an opportunity to express himself.

Get a large assortment of consumer magazines, some scissors, glue and poster board. Tell your consumer that you're interested in his impressions of a particular brand, let's say United Airlines. Ask him to cut out any pictures or words which express his sense of United's personality. The pictures can be of people, places or things.

Once he's finished cutting, ask him to arrange them on the board and glue them down. Ask him to describe why he chose the pictures he did and what they represent about United.

We've used this technique quite successfully on a variety of products and in a variety of situations. You can compare the collages of users and non-users of a brand, of heavy users and light users, male and female users, whatever makes sense in your given marketing situation. Consistently, we encounter an amazing richness of valuable insight into a consumer's perception of a brand.

Last, we'll talk about a technique which can be very useful for relating what a person wants out of life directly to the benefits a product can provide.

Laddering

Laddering is a structured process of questioning which connects the *attributes* or *characteristics* of a product to the *benefits* that product gives the consumer to the *values* those benefits serve in the customer's life.

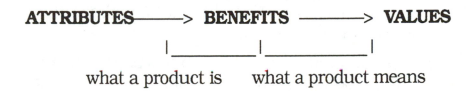

ATTRIBUTES———> BENEFITS ———> VALUES

what a product is   what a product means

113

Two-year-old children are naturally good at the laddering technique, because it's based on their favorite question–"Why?" Maybe you've even been "laddered" by a child once yourself. Here's an example.

You say, "It's getting late and it's time to go to bed."

The two-year-old asks, *"Why?"*

"Because tomorrow's a school day and you need your sleep."

"Why?"

"Because you need to be rested to do well in school."

"Why?"

"Because you need to get good grades so that someday you can go to college."

"Why?"

"Because if you go to college you can get a good job and take care of yourself."

"Why?"

"Because if you can take care of yourself, then you can take care of *me* when I get old!"

Assuming that you're willing to put up with a conversation like this, you can see that we started with a simple concrete fact "It's late and time to go to bed," and through a process of constantly asking *why*, we were able to find out how that fact is connected to a high level "value" in the parent's life, that is, being supported when she's old.

There are many other ways to climb this particular ladder, varying from, "So you can be President of the United States" to "Because you'll get a spanking if you don't stop asking so many stupid questions!"

The relationship between people and products or brands

can be pursued in the same way. You start with the "attributes" the consumer associates with a particular product.

"Attributes" are properties found in the product itself. They are tangible characteristics such as ingredients, color, price, shape, size or other meaningful features.

Asking a consumer "why" each of those attributes is important will yield the "benefits" each characteristic produces for the person. A "benefit" is what the product does for the consumer such as cleans brighter, saves time or lasts longer.

For example, if you ask a woman what characteristics are important to her in a moisturizer for her face, she may say that she wants it to be light and not greasy. If you ask her why that's important, she'll explain to you the "benefit"- that it keeps her face looking young and soft all day long.

Finally, asking "why" the benefit is important will give you the "value" it serves in the customer's life. A "value" is what the customer ultimately wants or needs from the product.

In the case of the skin moisturizer, our customer may say that she wants her face to look young and soft because she wants to feel and look young as long as she can. She doesn't intend to grow old gracefully, she intends to fight it all the way, as the advertising for Oil of Olay tells us.

An *attribute* is a property of a product.

A *benefit* is how a product relates to a person.

A *value* is a need internal to a person.

Here's an example of what a "ladder" might look like for Joy dishwashing detergent, and how Joy used it in their ads.

	Consumer	In Advertising
Attribute	Grease-cutting ingredients	"Lemony fresh"
Benefit	Gets dishes really clean	"Cleans down to the shine"
Value	I'm doing my home-making job well	"Isn't that a nice reflection on you"

Here's a ladder for Snickers candy bars. Again, the advertising connects the attributes of the brand to the needs or values of the consumer.

	Consumer	In Advertising
Attribute	Has lots of peanuts	"Packed with peanuts"
Benefit	Really fills me up	"Snickers really satisfies"
Value	I can concentrate when I'm not hungry	Between classes, you're hungry

Some Final Notes

In summary, it's impossible to predict how many days or weeks, how many interviews or how many ladders it will take you to get an insight into your consumers or your brand. Or exactly what sort of insight you might find.

Sometimes, a day in a supermarket makes it crystal clear, and sometimes you're in the third round of grueling focus groups and you still don't have a handle on it.

Sometimes, if you're first going into a category, you can have blinding insights in just a few hours. But, if you're working in a category that has been explored and analyzed at great length, beer for example, the task can be particularly daunting. Not that people won't be very insightful, but it seems like just about every insight there is has been tapped before.

But whatever situation you're in, enjoy the journey and push for your goal- a consumer insight that connects with a brand insight. The Sweet Spot.

PRINCIPLE IX

Talk to your customers, work hard on your questions, really listen to what they say. Use what you hear.

SECTION III
FROM INSIGHT TO INSPIRATION

Now you've done everything we've suggested and practiced every technique we've described. You've got more facts, anecdotes and experiences than you ever thought possible. You may even be a little overwhelmed. What now?

It's time to look at some concepts and structures that can help you organize what you've learned. These are the tools that can make your consumer insights clear. To yourself and to other members of the Planning team.

Here are the most useful:

1. **Perceptual Mapping**
2. **Segmentation**
3. **Hypothesis Testing**

These are by no means all the ways to organize what you know, but they're the most commonly used, and an excellent place to start.

13 MAPPING OUT PERCEPTIONS

"Beauty is in the eye of the beholder."
Margaret Wolfe Hungerford

Perceptual mapping is a good tool because it lets you draw what you know visually. It lets you take a great deal of information and look at it all at once. It lets you position one brand relative to others with respect to the dimensions that consumers use to distinguish them. Let's look at an example.

Soft Drinks

When people choose which soft drink to buy, of course they consider which flavor they're in the mood for and whether they want a diet or a regular soda. But if we've pushed a little deeper with our observations and interviews, we know that people actually drink the image and the heritage of a brand as well. (Something that Coca-Cola forgot when they introduced New Coke, as you may remember.)

So, if people drink the image and the heritage of a brand, what are the dimensions of that image, and what might the resulting map tell us about the opportunity for a brand we might be marketing?

Let's say you've learned that people associate some soft drinks as being for older people and others for younger people. Furthermore, there are some brands that people think of as traditional and others that are perceived as more innovative and unconventional.

If you treat each of these as an endpoint of an axis on a map, here's what you'll get.

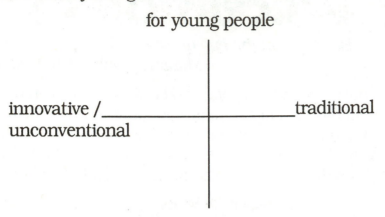

for young people

innovative /_____traditional
unconventional

for older people

Now, take the same map and fill in the various brands of soft drinks you can think of. Here's one person's opinion.

for young people

                              * Sunkist

innovative/_____ traditional
unconventional
                              *Pepsi

                        *7-UP

      * Diet Coke   * RC

        for older people   *Coke

One of the first things you'll notice is that most of the brands are clustered together in the "traditional/for older people" quadrant and that the "innovative/for young people" quadrant is empty. That's an insight.

There doesn't seem to be any brand that this person associated with being innovative and for young people. What if this person perceives himself as innovative and young? What is there then for him to drink?

Wait a minute, you may say, different brands have tried to get in that quadrant. And right you are. That's exactly where 7-UP tried to go with its "Uncola" campaign in the 70's. And that's exactly the destination they arrived at until they decided at some point that "Uncola" was out-of-date and it was time to try something else. By now, they've drifted back over to the lower right hand quadrant, at least in our hypothetical subject's mind.

Or, think about Dr. Pepper. This person hasn't even included Dr. Pepper on the map. But the wacky, outrageous advertising of the late 70's positioned the brand as young and innovative, challenging the viewer to "Be a Pepper." Since then, Dr. Pepper's marketing budgets have been slashed, and the brand has fallen completely off this person's map.

Now it's Pepsi's turn to try. "Pepsi. The Choice of a New Generation" is designed to get the brand up in the young, innovative quadrant and away from all the rest of the competition. That positioning along with a lot of other smart marketing has the brand neck and neck with Coke.

Maps are a lot of fun to put together, but they're hard work too. The dimensions that reveal the insights aren't always obvious and you may need to go through several tries before you find something that works.

For example, there are many other axes and quadrants you can use to map the soft drink category. Masculine/feminine, casual/sophisticated, country/city are just a few that might be helpful. And, of course, what "older" and "younger" mean depends on the age of the person you're interviewing. You might also want to see the differences in maps of Coke and Pepsi drinkers. Each time you draw a new map, another bit of insight can be revealed.

You can try mapping by the attributes, benefits and values you discovered in your laddering exercise. For example, an **Attribute Map** for the candy category might cross chocolate/non-chocolate and creamy/chewy with each other.

A **Benefit Map** for a household cleaner might cross gentle/strong-acting with convenient/time-consuming. And a **Value Map** for the wristwatch category might cross traditional/modern with popular/high status.

Or, you can make a **Combination Map**, crossing a benefit dimension with a value dimension as you might for the snack category: sweet/salty versus indulgent/spartan.

Get yourself a piece of paper, make a lot of empty "maps" and try to fill in the different dimensions that your consumers and your insights have told you distinguish one brand from another.

When you're done with your maps, ask yourself, "Which one of these is most useful? Which one crystallizes an idea for me? Which one can I show someone else to make what I've learned clear?"

And remember, once you've discovered your insight you have to use it to generate insight and inspiration in others.

14 SEGMENTING PEOPLE

"Blue, red, yellow and green are lovely colors when they're kept apart, but mix them altogether and you just get brown."
Anonymous

If you've spent much time talking to and observing consumers, chances are, you've probably felt overwhelmed by how different individual people can be. And while you always want to start the marketing process with an appreciation of people's differences, ultimately it helps to classify people into groups so that you can address your marketing efforts to the things they have in common.

Segmentation is also necessary for dealing with everyday life. The first segmentation scheme you ran across was probably in junior high or high school.

When I went to school, people were classified into several "types" by the other students. In my day, there were "greasers," "surfers" and "collegiates." The people in each type had more in common with each other than they did with people in any of the other types. They dressed alike, had the same interests and tastes, sat together in class and in the lunchroom, and spent most of their time outside class together.

Today, high school kids still use pretty much the same kind of caste classification system, but the names have changed. And new types have emerged as old types have wandered out of fashion. Last time I heard, there were "geeks," "burn-outs" and "preppies."

In many ways, the marketplace is just like high school.

When we market or advertise given brands, we need to classify people in order to deal with them more efficiently. People can be classified in a variety of ways, depending on the needs of a particular situation. That's a very important point for us to remember.

There is no one universally useful segmentation of people, no matter how hard we look for one. Instead, there are many ways to segment. You need to devise a segmentation tailored to your particular marketing situation.

A critical question to ask yourself is, "Is this way of classifying people meaningful and applicable?"

People can be classified according to many dimensions. Here are a few of the more common ways to group people.

Demographics. For instance: men vs. women, college educated vs. high school educated, high income vs. medium income vs. low income. People can be grouped according to any demographic characteristic.

Of course, you have to keep in mind that while demographic segmentation is very easy, it can be very superficial. Classifying beer drinkers by whether they are white collar or blue collar may miss motivations that are far more discriminating and far more meaningful.

Geographics. People can often be grouped geographically, by where they live. Not only are general regional classifications useful (Northerners, Midwesterners, Southerners, West Coasters), but a service called PRIZM has built a very successful business by grouping people according to their zip codes and demographics.

PRIZM's underlying theory is "birds of a feather flock together," and they do. If you think about the neighborhood you live in, you'll realize that the people who live in the homes and apartments around you are more like you than those who live several miles away. PRIZM has forty zip code clusters with names like "Money and Brains," "Urban Gold Coast," and "Young Influentials."

Behavior. You can classify people by something they do. For example, by a sport in which they participate: runners vs. weight lifters vs. skiers. By how they like to spend their time.

A number of years ago, Leo Burnett did a study of tennis players for Wilson Sporting Goods. They found that the market could be classified by the consumer's involvement in tennis as a sport. They found 30% beginners, 25% socializers (people who liked tennis as a social activity), 25% competitors (people who didn't want just to play, but to *win*) and 20% at the top of the market they called buffs.

You can imagine that the appeal Wilson used to reach these people might vary according to the specific segment they were trying to reach. And, not only might Wilson advertise differently to each segment, they might also create different products to address the particular needs of each. And each segment would have a different Sweet Spot, so to speak.

Product Use. This is a very common way of segmenting people. It's not always the most useful, as it tends to view people only from the point-of-view of the manufacturer. Some examples include: category users vs. non-users; brand X vs. brand Y vs. brand Z users; loyal users vs. brand switchers.

And, it can certainly be useful.

Segmenting the coffee market into ground roast users and instant coffee users was useful for both Folger's and Taster's Choice. They recognized that while instant coffee users appreciated the convenience of instant, they also felt that the product they used was inferior in flavor and aroma.

Both Folger's and Taster's Choice have used that insight to good advantage, by creating new products that come close to the "ground roast standard" that instant users perceive to be a most important consideration.

Attitudes. You can group people according to an attitude or opinion they have in common. For example: liberals vs. conservatives, environmentally concerned vs. unconcerned.

Lifestyle and Values. This type of segmentation was made famous by VALS (Values and Lifestyles). As we described in an earlier chapter, VALS classifies consumers into one of nine types, according to the values and lifestyles they share.

You can gain many valuable insights into many markets using Values segmentations. The car market is one good example. Chevrolet, for instance, positions its products to the values of the mainstream "belonger" with the themeline "The Heartbeat of America." BMW makes its cars consistent with the values of an "achiever" audience by calling itself "The Ultimate Driving Machine." And Volvo aims at the lifestyle and values of the "societally conscious" with "A Car You Can Believe In."

A Word of Caution

While segmentations can be very useful tools, it's often easy to fall into the trap of thinking that the research segments take the place of people themselves.

For instance, it's easy to stereotype people and believe that they *are* "belongers" or "achievers" rather than realize these are simply labels for grouping consumers with varied char-acteristics according to what they seem to have in common.

For that reason, it's still best to get to know your customers as individual people before you try to segment them. If you do it that way, you're a lot less likely to make the critical error of oversimplifying them.

Benefit Segmentation

Finally, you can sort people according to the benefits the product you're studying gives them. Here's an exercise I often use to help people create a segmentation like that.

Next time you're in a drugstore with a large candy aisle, buy yourself one of everything. Buy some candy bars, hard candies of various types, chocolate covered peanuts, raisins and M&Ms. Buy some jelly beans, caramels, and some chocolate and non-chocolate mints. Then buy some chocolate covered cherries or other candies that come in a box.

When you get home, eat it all. (Just kidding.) Pour the bulk of the goodies out on a table and sort it. Immediately you'll realize that there are lots of ways to group the candy: flavor, size, packaging, ingredients, price, brand name or manufacturer, etc.

All of those can be very useful segmentations, depending on the marketing situation. For purposes of this exercise, sort the candies by the *way you might eat them.*. Think about the situations in which you eat each different type, how and why you eat it, and how you feel when you do it.

When most people do this exercise, here's what they seem to come up with.

Indulgent Candies. Candies you really concentrate on and savor. Ones that taste rich and make you feel special and indulged. Ones that you save for special occasions or give as gifts to special friends or relatives. For example: boxed chocolate and thin, fancy chocolate bars.

Hunger Satisfiers. Candies you eat as a snack between meals. Candies that fill you up and keep you from getting hungry, like in the mid-afternoon. Candies that make you feel like you've eaten something substantial. For example: big candy bars, chunky candy bars and the like.

Compulsive Candies. Candies you eat by the handful or more, like popcorn. Once you get started, you usually eat the whole bag. Candies you eat while you're doing something else. For example: M&Ms, chocolate covered peanuts and raisins, jelly beans, candy corn.

Candies That Keep You Company. Little candies you eat one at a time. Something you can suck on for a while. Candies that cheer you up. A little treat you can give yourself when you're tired or bored. Candies you can offer to other people to make them feel welcome. For example: hard candy of all flavors, individually wrapped caramels or jellied candy.

Meal Finishers. Something you eat at the end of a meal that makes you feel the meal is really complete. Candies that psychologically satisfy you at the end of a meal. For example: mints of all kinds, and such.

If you were a candy manufacturer, what would you do with information from a segmentation like this one? One of the things I would do is cross-tabulate each "benefit segment" by the type of candy in it, the volume of candy in it, the share of various brands, and by the demographics of the people in each segment. Then I'd look to see where I compete, and if there are holes in my product line I should fill in.

Here's an example.

Segmentation	Type of Candy	Leading Brand
Indulgent	Boxed chocolate	Whitman's
Satisfiers	Candy bars	Mars
Compulsive	Pieces	M&Ms
Company	Non-chocolate	Brach's
Finishers	Mints	Andes

The Product Adoption Curve

The last segmentation scheme we want to discuss is one which is especially helpful when you're introducing new products. It's called the "product adoption curve" or the "innovation curve." The work to develop and test this tool was done by Everett Rogers and is described in a book called *The Diffusion of Innovation.*

The premise behind the adoption curve is that different people adopt new ideas or try new products at different times. Some people like to be the first to try something new and other people want to wait a bit to see if it catches on before they try it, and still others will only accept a new product or idea after it's been around a long, long time.

Consider how you feel about new products. Were you one of the first people to buy a CD player, or did you want to wait to see if it really caught on? Did you buy a cellular phone when they first came out, or did you wait 'til the price came down? Do you use a computer at work, or would you rather wait until everyone else is using one before you learn? Do you change your hemlines as soon as the fashion magazines suggest, or do you wait for your peers?

Rogers describes five types of people who vary depending on how open they make themselves to new innovations. He calls them "Innovators," "Early Adopters," "Early Majority," "Late Majority" and "Laggards."

Innovators. Innovators always want to be the first to try something new. They tend to be very adventurous people. They don't mind taking risks even when it means making an occasional mistake. To them, it's more important to be first than to be right. If you bought colored contact lenses as soon as they came out, you're probably an innovator.

Early Adopters. Early adopters wait until a product has been around a short while, but they don't want to be far behind the leading edge. Early adopters are usually opinion leaders for other people and often know a great deal about a category. Perhaps you didn't buy the first microwave on the market, but rather waited until the bugs had been worked out and the price came down a little bit. If that describes your general behavior as a consumer, then you're probably an early adopter.

Early Majority. People in the early majority are very deliberate about when, and if, they try a new product or idea. They're more cautious than the early adopters, although they're still open to new ideas. They weren't the first people to buy CD players, for example, but once their friends had them and well-known companies were making them, they decided it was time to take the plunge.

Late Majority. People in this group are usually skeptical about new products and ideas and wait until a product is well-established before trying it. They may not even try it until they get pressure from their friends or family. These are probably people just getting ready to buy their first VCR.

Laggards. These are the very last people to try a new idea. Often their economic circumstances prevent them from trying something until it is very well-established and the price comes down. Or they could just be cheap. More than that, they tend to be very traditional in their outlook on life and don't really see the point of changing the "tried and true" ways of doing things. Like my grandmother, who didn't buy an automatic coffee maker until 1985.

Besides describing each of these types of people, Rogers shows how many of them there are in the population.

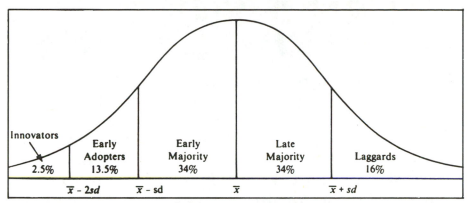

Do people adopt new products at different rates in the category you're studying? If they do, then you'll probably find this segmentation useful for knowing how to introduce a new product, to whom and when.

There is also some empirical evidence that the curve is going faster. VCR's and FAX's are examples of fairly rapid adoption curves. Think how quickly you "adopted" CNN during the Persian Gulf crisis.

All of these segmenting techniques represent useful ways of organizing people's behavior and a product's benefit.

These techniques, plus your own hard work, can help you find exactly the insights you're looking for.

PRINCIPLE X

Organize your insights in a way that makes them clear and easy to understand.
Use a map, a segmentation or a model.

15 HOW TO KNOW AN INSIGHT WHEN YOU SEE ONE

"My overall advice...is to relax a little and to differentiate between pure hunch...and conditioned intuition."

Leo Burnett

We've talked about insight throughout this whole book- watching for the insight, pushing for the insight, discovering the insight, etc. But what exactly *is* an insight? What is a Consumer Insight? What is a Brand Insight? Where's this magical Sweet Spot we've been describing? How do you know one when you run across one in a dark alley?

While we can't tell you what insight you'll arrive at in your particular case, we can give you a few hints and guidelines that may help you know when you're there.

1. You'll Know It When You See It

"Eureka!" "That's it!" In our business, we respond at an almost electric level when we make a significant new connection or recognize an important pattern.

Probably, it's the same feeling a chimpanzee has when he suddenly discovers that by grabbing the stick he's been playing with and climbing on a nearby stump, he is able to knock down a tasty banana for himself.

If you're excited and what you've learned seems like a revelation to you (and to other people, too) then there's a good chance you've probably found the Sweet Spot.

Working on Durasoft Colors contact lenses, which can change your eyes from one color to any other (even from brown to blue), the agency researchers interviewed many, many women. They spoke with the women about how they felt about clothes, cosmetics and haircoloring- all kinds of

132

consumer products that help one change one's appearance or improve one's overall image.

The women spoke of how much fun it was to play around with clothes and make-up, to be one person one day and a different person another day. This told us something about their consumer personalities. Then they tried the lenses and saw for themselves the dramatic change they could produce.

One woman said, *"This is fantastic. You know, up to this point we've had the power to change anything about ourselves, anything but our eye color. You can change your hair color, the shape of your nose, the size of your hips, the color of your fingernails. But your eye color was something you couldn't change. Now we even have power over that."*

Suddenly an eye-opening insight! The researcher involved remarked, *"This product isn't about fun and playing around at all. It's about power. The power to control yourself. The power to make yourself be exactly what you want to be!"*

A simple commercial, demonstrating the power to change your eye color from one color to any other- *"and that kind of power can be a dangerous thing,"* hit the insight dead on. In their first year of introduction, Durasoft Colors sold in record-breaking numbers.

2. It Will Have a Simplicity and Elegance, Connecting With a Number of Pieces of Data

An insight will often explain a lot of the facts you've found with a wonderful, unifying simplicity. You'll say to yourself, *"Now I truly understand how all those facts and figures I've gathered fit together in the bigger picture."*

The graduate students at Northwestern University were assigned a project in a Consumer Behavior class to uncover some insight into the much talked-about "Twentysomething" generation. After a tremendous amount of fact-finding and research, they concluded that instead of being confused, alienated and despondent people, the way the media frequently portray them, young people today were trying to forge a new way through life, outside a system that doesn't take care of them the way it took care of their parents.

The insight: They don't reject the "Establishment," they simply find it irrelevant to their needs.

"Now we understand," the students said, "why people are marrying later, not voting as much, not attending church, starting their own businesses, and refusing to be 'loyal' in the traditional sense to their companies." It's not that they reject the values that those institutions stand for, they simply don't find that buying in to them helps them on the road they think they have to travel in life.

3. Sometimes the Best Insight Is No Insight At All

You'll find this is true particularly in commodity categories or in categories where insights have been mined for years.

Batteries are a good example.

While working on the Energizer account for Chiat/Day, the Account Planners discovered that they could not find a meaningful alternative to the "long-lasting" position dominated by Duracell, the category leader.

The insight? That they had to take on Duracell directly. Outlast the longest-lasting. Simple.

The commercial spoofs starring the pink bunny are certainly memorable. And they make the point that nothing outlasts the Energizer. Now that they plan to use the bunny on the packaging so that people don't have to remember the brand name, Energizer advertising should make an even greater impact.

4. When It's Executed,
It Has the Power to Move People

And, yes, that means sometimes you don't know you've hit an insight until after the fact, until it's executed.

Here's another way to think about the same thing.

Have you ever received a present at some point in your life that, when you opened it, made you feel wonderful, completely understood, respected and loved? You thought to yourself, *"This person understands what I'm all about"*?

It happened to me when I was 12 or 13 and had aspirations of becoming a fine cook someday. It wasn't something that I talked much about, only having learned how to section grapefruits in 7th grade home ec. class. But anyone who was really paying attention to me could probably tell. And, someone was paying attention.

For Christmas that year, my aunt gave me a cookbook. Not just an ordinary cookbook– the _Great Chefs Cookbook_, filled with all sorts of gourmet recipes by all sorts of elite people made with a lot of ingredients I'd never even heard of. But I'll never forget the idea it communicated to me. I thought, here's someone who understands me, who believes in me and cares about me. My aunt's present had hit my Sweet Spot.

That's the same thing that happens to a consumer when your product, ad or marketing idea draws on the insight you've discovered and hits the Sweet Spot. (Although it might not be quite as sentimental.)

It's how the early Lee Jeans ads made me feel. It's how the introduction of the Gillette Sensor razor made millions of men all over the world feel. It's what the Mazda Miata makes its driver feel. It's what Apple Computer and its advertising make its target feel.

"Somebody Understands Me"

Discovering an insight, however, isn't a guessing game. It is an intuitive leap from a solid foundation of information. In that sense, you can think of it as *an informed intuition*.

But, because it's an informed intuition, a little more information may help you out, particularly if you're not sure you're there yet.

It's time for some hypothesis testing.

16 HYPOTHESIS TESTING

*"The construction of hypotheses is a creative act
of inspiration, intuition, invention."*

Milton Friedman

As we've said, if you have a good insight, you'll also find a lot of evidence to support it. This section is about testing the soundness of your insight.

Think about your insight as an hypothesis. That's all it really is– an idea about why people behave the way they do in a given circumstance. If your hypothesis is good, you'll be able to predict the evidence which will corroborate it. If not, you'll find evidence which contradicts it.

Let's work through an example.

You're working on the advertising for a company in the medical services area. Now, suppose that, based on your interviews and observations, your insight is that people should be segmented according to their relationships with their physicians. Let's say you've identified three types of people: "Dependents," "Partners" and "Independents."

"Dependents" are people who are totally dependent on their doctors. They don't question what their doctors say and they do whatever they're told. They don't believe they have much control over their health and are consequently fatalistic. They don't believe there's much point to trying to prevent illness. They go to a doctor when they're sick and leave it to him or her to fix the problem.

"Independents" have very little faith in doctors or traditional medicine. They believe that their health is fully their responsibility and may use doctors as a source of information, but not their only source. They believe good health is a matter of their own control and so they tend to focus on prevention.

"Partners" fall somewhere in between. They're people who treat their doctors as peers and equals. They trust and respect their doctors, but don't blindly follow everything they say. They expect to be told what's wrong, why, how to fix it and how to prevent it in the future. They feel responsible for the state of their health, but in the end, they hold the doctor responsible as well.

You think your client should target "Partners" and aim the advertising at that group's Sweet Spot.

Now based on these insights, let's make a few predictions.

1. Who do you think is most likely to subscribe to *Prevention* magazine?
2. Who is most likely to smoke, drink or be overweight?
3. Who is most likely to want to have a baby at home with a midwife?
4. Who is most likely to be following the American Cancer Society's guidelines and the American Heart Association's guidelines?
5. Who consumes the most vitamins?
6. Who watches the medical programming on *Lifetime* cable?
7. Who's likely to rely on a single doctor as opposed to having a stable of specialists?
8. Who's likely to be oldest? The best educated?
9. What happens to each type if he or she gets a serious disease?
10. Can you classify yourself as predominantly one of these three types? How about your parents or your friends?

Can you predict the answer to each of the questions?

1. "Independents" are most likely to subscribe to *Prevention.*
2. "Dependents" tend to smoke, drink and be overweight.
3. "Independents" tend to want to have a baby at home.
4. "Partners" are most likely to follow the ACA and AHA guidelines.
5. "Independents" consume the most vitamins.
6. "Independents" watch medical programming. "Partners" watch a program if they have the specific problem being discussed.
7. "Dependents" tend to have a single doctor.
8. "Dependents" are the oldest."Partners" and "Independents" are the best-educated.
9. "Dependents" get more dependent."Partners" get better informed. "Independents" seek out alternative medical solutions.

In a large scale, quantitative study designed to confirm or disconfirm this segmentation, the sample was asked the above questions. Sure enough, the different groups behaved just as they were predicted to behave, and the segmentation was deemed sound enough to use as a basis for marketing and advertising decisions.

On the other hand, sometimes your hypothesis needs a little refinement. Maybe it doesn't explain all the facts, or doesn't explain them very well.

For example, a group of research people were doing some investigation into young men's perspectives on their lives to help a men's magazine refine its target. In the beginning, they thought a segmentation that divided men into two basic groups would be enough: those who wanted control over their lives, and those willing to give that control over to someone or something else.

As the interviewing of young men progressed, they found they were missing something. The men who wanted to keep control was too big a group. It included just about everyone. They realized there were really two kinds of men combined in the group: those with a vision of exactly what they wanted in life and believed they were responsible for getting themselves there; and those who were more opportunistic, wanting the freedom to take advantage of unforseen opportunities as they came along. Both wanted control, but they wanted to exert it in different ways.

With that additional insight, they invented a new segmentation and used a metaphor about driving to describe it. They decided some men were "drivers with maps," others were "drivers without maps," and the third group, willing to take life totally as it came, they called "passengers."

To check themselves one more time, they asked themselves, "If this segmentation is true, what else should be true?" They thought that each segment of men ought to admire different kinds of people, each should have a different kind of hero.

So back to the field they went– and asked one more question. *Who are the people you admire?*

Sure enough, they found something very interesting. The "drivers with maps" admired people like Churchill and Iacocca. They liked to read biographies of famous men, and one of their all-time favorite movies was "Patton."

The "drivers without maps" had a different sort of hero. They tended to like movies like "Dances with Wolves" and "Field of Dreams," and to admire people who took what opportunities came along and made the most of them- like Arnold Schwartzenegger.

The "passengers" were a different sort altogether. They tended to enjoy pure escapist and fantasy movies, and to admire friends who lived day-to-day and didn't succumb to pressure from the "Establishment" to put down roots.

Thus satisfied that their segmentation worked, they felt they could move on to marketing recommendations to their client.

Once you have your insight, ask yourself, "If my idea is true, what else should also be true?" Then search out the proof.

PRINCIPLE XI

Test out your hypotheses.

Make sure they fit the facts.

17 FOSTERING AND INSPIRING COLLABORATION

"Advertising is a team sport."

Bruce Bendinger

Your investment is starting to pay off. You now have an insight into your customers. You've watched them, spent time with them and talked to them. You've learned to see things from their point-of-view. You've organized what you know into a segmentation or a theory that makes sense.

You've tested out your ideas and found some corroboration and support. You've got an insight into your brand. You're pretty sure you've found the Sweet Spot.

Congratulations. But your insights won't do any good if no one else on the marketing team will work with them. And you'll find that sometimes happens.

In theory, the results should speak for themselves and everyone else should, quite logically, get with the program. Well, we all know the real world doesn't always work that way.

Our insights are seldom proven beyond a shadow of a doubt. So, while understanding the consumer and turning information into insight is a tough task, your job's not over.

In fact, it moves to a whole new level, where teamwork and interaction work with the core insight and further develop it into a great marketing or advertising execution.

To make sure your insights don't simply fall by the wayside, you need to do two things.

1. **Encourage everyone on your team to work together, with the customer in mind.**

2. **Make your insight inspire them.**

We'll spend this last chapter on those two issues.

The Importance of Collaboration

Over the last twenty years, marketing and advertising have evolved into fields with highly specialized functions.

In advertising agencies, there are some people who specialize in media, research, creative and account management.

In manufacturing and service companies, there are people who specialize in new product development, sales training, pricing, research, sales promotion, package design, corporate communications and brand management.

While all of these activities are necessary to the final marketing or advertising product, no individual completes or controls the entire process. Consequently, we repeatedly run up against the problem of how to get a group of people with different backgrounds, functions and agendas all working toward the same goal.

That was not always the case. In the beginning, people like Leo Burnett or Claude Hopkins were virtually "full service" advertising and marketing people all by themselves. They developed strategy, created the advertising, invented promotion ideas, named products, fashioned packages, offered up new product ideas and worked on media plans. All the while, they had the "client contact."

It's much more rare to find anyone like that these days. Marketing and advertising are a lot more complicated and technical than they used to be. We have to work together.

An additional frustration working in marketing or advertising stems from the problems of cooperating with other people. Walk into any advertising agency and you'll probably hear remarks like these.

Researcher: *"I know what the prospects for this brand need to hear. Why won't the creative people make ads aimed at them instead of at the awards judges?"*

Art Director: *"We've got a great advertising idea here that only works as a two-page spread. Why can't the media people just fix the plan to accommodate it? Isn't this agency really serious about wanting great advertising?"*

Account Manager: *"If I've told them once, I've told them a hundred times. Who cares if they think it's great advertising? The client won't buy it. What are we supposed to do? Sacrifice our whole relationship with these people over one ad?"*

Media Planner: *"I've planned for all 30-second spots. That's what maximizes the client's budget. Why should we sacrifice half the frequency to accommodate some 60 -second idea?"*

Client: *"Don't these people care that I've got sales goals to meet this quarter? Why don't they just help me?"*

Each person has a point, the way he or she sees it. But, as much as most people wish it weren't so, working with other people is a fact of life. No one gets the job done by himself.

Let's assume that you have those five different people, each with his or her own agenda, all of whom are necessary to get something done. What would you do?

Here's a list of some of the solutions people have proposed.

1. Put the client foremost and make everyone do only the work he or she will buy.
2. Put the creative director in charge and teach everyone else how to sell the work the creative teams develop.

3. Put the account manager in charge and let her be the gatekeeper between the agency and the client.

4. Obey the media plan. Whatever you do, make sure it conforms to the media department's computer.

5. Establish some balance of power between the account manager and the creative director and treat everyone else as support staff.

6. Put everyone in a room and let them hash it out until they come up with a solution that's satisfactory to everyone.

For every solution we've listed above, there's an advertising agency which tries to solve the problem of cooperation by organizing itself in that way. And, while the work usually gets done, the process is rarely satisfying to anyone involved. Even to the person whose "rules" are in effect.

The same can be said for many other businesses as well. Sales, production and finance are three powerful functions that often end up operating at cross-purposes. Conflicts often arise between the home office and the branch office, the employer and the employee.

In every business of every size there are groups and individuals with very different agendas and priorities.

Yet, as we will discuss, there is something that can work to unify them all: *the customer.*

Compromise Vs. Collaboration

Any activity which requires the participation of a number of people depends on cooperation to get the job done. We have to work together to get anywhere.

There are two basic ways we can cooperate:*compromise* and *collaboration.*

Unfortunately, most of the time, we end up compromising instead of collaborating. Compromise happens when individuals start the process of cooperation with their own personal needs and agendas in mind. Each person gradually trades off his own individual objectives against every other person's individual objectives until the group can agree on something everyone can live with.

You've probably been in situations such as that. Every marketing and advertising person, it seems, has experienced a time when their ad, or research report or marketing strategy or package design was ground up by the mill of compromise. Little else can be accomplished by compromise.

The phrase "a camel is a horse designed by a committee" accurately describes what compromise usually achieves. This can even last until the commercial is shot, where the director is often asked to "shoot it both ways."

Being familiar with frustration of the process and the generally unsatisfactory results, most marketing and advertising people try to avoid compromise. However, what they may end up doing is completely evading any kind of cooperation as well. Cooperation becomes equivalent to compromise and an advertising "team" can often be anything but.

Many marketing or advertising people will tell you that everything would be fine if they just didn't have to deal with anyone else and could do the whole thing alone. And, to the best of their abilities, that's what they try to do. Keep everyone else out.

146

That process rarely serves anyone's individual interest, let alone the marketing or advertising product. It's in everyone's best interest to find a better way.

And there is a better way. It's called *collaboration.*

Collaboration happens when every participant is focused on *the objective they all have in common* and brings to bear his or her special talents and skills to achieve it. When people have a shared goal, they can feel responsible to that common objective first and their individual agendas second. "One for all, and all for one."

What should be the common objective of everyone involved in any aspect of marketing and/or advertising? Obviously, we think that finding a way to hit the consumers's Sweet Spot is an excellent shared goal.

And, in fact, every business writer and thinker from Peter Drucker to Tom Peters talks about some sort of consumer focus. *"Launch a Customer Revolution,"* says Tom Peters, *"...look at the smallest nuance of the tiniest program through the customer's eyes."*

We agree.

Focusing on hitting the customer's Sweet Spot doesn't preclude getting a tremendous amount of personal satisfaction from your strategic work or media plans or even from winning an award or two for the advertising. It doesn't preclude profits or necessarily cost more. In fact, things are likely to work more profitably precisely because you've worked first to make your efforts resonate with the consumer.

Collaboration is very hard work. And it's not work that seems very natural to most people, at least at first. It's not a process that most of us have been trained to use effectively in the execution of our daily business.

But if you can, you'll find that your frustration with working in groups will decrease and your satisfaction with the results you produce will improve tremendously. And, once people learn to work this way, it can be invigorating, enjoyable and very productive. You end up with "team spirit" and everyone working toward a common goal.

INSPIRING COLLABORATION

Collaboration, as we've said, is a difficult process, especially at first. It's one that has to be closely guarded, fostered and shepherded. Everyone involved has to actively support it all the time for it to have any chance to work.

Collaboration begins with an expressed willingness to respect the particular skills and talents every participant brings to the table. That's often a major hurdle to overcome. Ask yourself, *"Do I really respect the other people I work with and depend on every day?"* Be honest with yourself.

If you're a talented creative person, do you really respect the research people you work with? If you're an account management person, do you really respect what the client has to offer? If you're a brand manager, do you really respect the writers and art directors you work with? If you're a student, do you really respect the other people you work with in group projects? And your professor?

Chances are, there's at least a part of you that doesn't. And there are probably a few co-workers who aren't on your list of All-Time Favorite People.

Why is that? Are these people totally unskilled or talentless? Maybe sometimes. But, more often, it's because we simply don't know the people we work with very well. Consequently we can't relate to them very easily. And, not surprisingly, we have difficulty persuading them.

148

This is the same problem we often have with consumers. We don't know our colleagues as *people* very well at all.

Here's where the consumer insight techniques you've been practicing throughout this book can come in handy.

You can use precisely the same techniques you used to get insight into consumers to get insight into your fellow collaborators. And you can use that insight as a way to connect with them, *just the same way you would with any other consumer.* You have to find their Sweet Spots, too.

So spend some time learning about the other people on your team. Observe them and talk to them. Find out what they like best and least about their jobs. What do they consider their greatest success and their worst failure? What do they think is the most satisfying work they've ever done? What are they most proud of? Who do they admire? What advertising or which marketing programs do they wish they had been responsible for?

Learning what motivates your fellow workers will help you find a way to help them focus on the consumer.

Knowing them as people is a vital first step on the road to productive collaboration.

Presentations That Inspire

The final area we'll consider is how to present what you know to someone else– one of the ways we communicate and persuade in the daily grind of advertising and marketing.

For example, how do you present research findings to creative people? How do you present advertising to a brand manager? How do you present an advertising or marketing objective and strategy to the whole team?

We're all very interested in making better presentations. So much of what we do in the marketing and advertising business requires sharp presentation skills. And I suspect that many of you may have taken presentation skills classes or read a few books on the topic.

One day, not too long ago, I asked the students in my class how many had ever taken a presentation skills workshop. Most of them had. I asked them what were the main things they learned. Here's what they said.

1. Maintain good eye contact.
2. Speak forcefully and confidently.
3. Smile.
4. Don't fidget and stand still.
5. Don't stand in front of your charts or other props.
6. Speak to your audience. Don't read off of your presentation materials.

All of these are good presentation tips. But for me, they fall into the category of "presentation hygiene." They're the things that can help make your presentations smooth, but they're not the things that can make them inspiring.

So I asked the question another way. Have you ever heard a presentation that really *inspired* you? What was it like? Here's what they said.

1. The speaker really understood what I was thinking about.
2. I learned something I could use.
3. The speaker explained something in a way that I could understand.
4. The enthusiasm of the presentation was so compelling I walked away excited and eager to get going.

As you can see, there's a marked difference between the first set of answers and the second.

The first set focuses on things *the speaker* does and the second focuses on the *effect the speaker had on the listener.*

(For more good insights on this, you might want to take a look at *"The Responsive Chord,"* by Tony Schwartz.)

A good presentation is like a good ad. It hits your Sweet Spot. The "breakthrough" is people becoming involved in what you have to say, because then they can read opportunities for their success in your story.

So, if you want the other people on the marketing or advertising team to focus on the consumer or make use of the other work you've produced, you have to find a way to target and hit their Sweet Spot too.

You have to take into account their needs and motivations. And you have to take into account how they learn. Are they more "right brain" or more "left brain?"

Do they learn best with numbers or words or pictures? You have to deliver your message in a form they can easily digest. Just like with any good ad.

The form may be different depending on the person you're talking to. A creative person may think and learn differently from a client. You may have to change your presentation a great deal to take those differences into account.

Different audiences. Different benefits. Different Sweet Spots. Adjust your presentation.

And you may think this all sounds like a lot of hard and time-consuming work. But think of the alternative. You go to all the trouble of having an insight, only to have it go unused because you didn't work hard enough to make it connect with someone else.

An Example

At an advertising agency I once worked for, we gave a presentation to a bank client to convince him to target a segment of people in addition to the one he usually targeted. For him, a banker concerned with segment size and profitability, we prepared a presentation that constructed our argument on a variety of calculations that showed the size of the segment, the current and lifetime profitability of the segment, and the neighborhoods around the bank in which these customers could be found.

We showed him how their Sweet Spot could be hit with a special savings program that helped the target save for college. The client was convinced and gave us the go-ahead.

The presentation to the creative team was a different matter entirely. Here, we showed them the results of a comprehensive ethnography study, complete with slides of the people we interviewed, the houses they lived in and the lives they led. We also put together a videotape of these people talking about their hopes and fears are for their children as they reach college age.

Finally, we collected a short reel of TV commercials that talked about life and products the way the target liked to think about them- commercials that hit their Sweet Spot in other categories so that the creative team could see some pictures and hear some music that might inspire them.

It worked. The creative team left the presentation inspired and eager to create. The work they produced sold to the client on the first presentation. And the bank started opening special savings programs for college tuition.

Another Example

Even when you present only to your client, you may have to make several different presentations.

The marketing manager may have a completely different

Sweet Spot than the CEO. The sales force often has another Sweet Spot entirely. And you have to accomodate each.

For a beer brand that I once worked on, we discovered we could persuade the marketing manager by showing him all the different creative ideas we had explored and by taking him through all the nuances of each execution and the thought process we had used to finally get to our recommendation.

On the other hand, the CEO would never put up with such a meandering presentation. All he wanted to see was our final recommendation. Clean and crisp. No "fluff and nonsense." He wanted to read the scripts himself and be shown the research that backed it up.

The distributors, on the other hand, had to be pumped up. We'd start off our presentation by working them up into a fever against the competition. Then, we provoked their curiosity with a "teaser" ad for our new campaign. After we'd finally showed them the work, we turned our tagline into a rallying cry and revealed a contest with prizes for the most sales.

To each his own.

Next time you make a presentation, think hard about what it takes to get the point across. How does your audience have to hear it to be inspired by it? Where is their Sweet Spot? How can you best connect with it?

If you can express your insights in a way they can absorb, chances are, they'll walk out of the room eager to hit the consumer's Sweet Spot too.

They'll be eager because they'll sense how hitting that spot can lead to their own success.

The Role of the Consumer "Advocate"

We're all familiar with people like Ralph Nader who are consumer advocates-at-large. They're people who fight for the rights of every person to have access to good, safe products at a fair value.

Every marketing and advertising group needs a different kind of a "consumer advocate" who asks, *"is this ad, package, media vehicle, pricing strategy, new product, etc. in the best interests of our consumer? Does it make use of what insights we have about that person? Does it communicate? Does it hit the Sweet Spot?"*

Being the "consumer advocate" sometimes means asking the tough questions. Mike Miles, now the CEO of Phillip Morris, filled that role when he was at Kentucky Fried Chicken. He put himself in the customer's shoes and asked himself and everyone else: Are these stores really clean and inviting enough? When the answer was no, Mike Miles set out to make things better.

More recently, at Kraft, Miles encouraged some new brand insights on Cheez-Whiz™. Was this a cheese spread that had been around for years? Or was it a great new cheese sauce for the microwave?

Some of these insights may be as old as "the customer Is always right," or even "do unto others..." But today, we have to work harder than ever to hear our customers over the noise of the modern marketplace. And we have to work harder than ever to help everyone on our team hear our customer as well.

Why Everyone Should Be A Consumer Advocate

As you'll see in the final section of this book, in some advertising agencies which operate according to this philosophy, the "consumer advocate" is called an "account planner."

But, the job doesn't have to be the responsibility of just one person. Ideally, it's the responsibility of *each and every one of us* involved in the business of marketing and advertising.

Nordstrom, again, is a good example of consumer advocacy in action. Every sales associate knows that to the customer, he or she *is* Nordstrom. Whether it's calling the customer to let her know an item is in, running to another department to find an accessory that coordinates with an outfit, or writing a note to thank her for her purchase, a Nordstrom sales associate does what it takes. *That's* Consumer Advocacy. The customer isn't just "always right," the customer is *all!*

At this point, we should also mention that the role of consumer advocate can be slightly intoxicating (representing the consumer can be heady stuff). The trick here is to represent the consumer *point-of-view* and get everyone involved to focus on the consumer, not on you.

Gaining insight into your consumer is a job where everyone can contribute. From Research Assistant to CEO. And if you approach consumers sensitively, respectfully, and intelligently, it doesn't require a Ph.D. in consumer behavior to make that contribution productive.

PRINCIPLE XII

Foster collaboration. Be a consumer advocate.

Today, it's tougher than ever. Competition is tougher and smarter, and consumers have many choices.

But it can be done. Whatever you want to accomplish, knowing your consumers will help you win in the marketplace.

In business after business, a drive to know the consumer has resulted in victory- a winning campaign, a winning marketing plan, a winning new product, a winning business.

And, after all, we all want to be winners.

TWELVE PRINCIPLES OF CONSUMER INSIGHT

PRINCIPLE I

Consumer Insight + Brand Insight= Sweet Spot

PRINCIPLE II

You don't persuade people. They persuade themselves.

PRINCIPLE III

The first step toward success is placing yourself in your customer's shoes.

PRINCIPLE IV

If you want to understand your customers, the best place to start is by understanding yourself.

PRINCIPLE V

Get the facts. When you're exploring a new marketplace, make sure your insights are grounded on facts.

PRINCIPLE VI

DATA–>INFORMATION–>INSIGHT–>*INSPIRATION*

156

PRINCIPLE VII
Little clues often reveal big insights.

PRINCIPLE VIII
You'll know consumers better in their natural setting.

PRINCIPLE IX
Talk to your customers, work hard on your questions,
really listen to what they say. Use what you hear.

PRINCIPLE X
Organize your insights in a way that makes them
clear and easy to understand.
Use a map, a segmentation or a model.

PRINCIPLE XI
Test out your hypotheses. Make sure they fit the facts.

PRINCIPLE XII
Foster collaboration. Be a consumer advocate.

SECTION IV
CONSUMER INSIGHT AT WORK

This section is about how the principles in this book translate into particular jobs.

First, we discuss the account planning "revolution" and the role of the account planner in advertising and marketing.

Then we asked a number of successful individuals– from agency researchers to small business owners– to tell us how the principles in the book help them do their own jobs.

Each individual shows us how Consumer Insight helped them be more successful in today's more competitive than ever business world.

We'd like to thank all of those who took time from their busy jobs to share their own insights with us.

We hope they inspire you.

18 THE ACCOUNT PLANNING REVOLUTION

One of the newest roles in advertising is Account Planning. The account planner's job is to bring the philosophy of Consumer Insight to life within an advertising agency.

The account planner is a person who actively works to understand the consumer and explain him or her to the other members of the agency team.

Some have described the role as adding passion and intuition to traditional agency research. Others say it's simply consumer research done the way it should be done.

In many cases, the account planner has proven to be an important addition to the traditional agency team. This was particularly true in England, where Account Planning began.

Today, the account planner is a valuable partner at many agencies in many countries. Often, the planner is a valuable member of agency management.

In the U.S., Account Planning can best be seen at Chiat/Day/Mojo, which has used it extensively since the early 80s.

Jay Chiat attributes much of his agency's success to the way they use Account Planning to provide their Creative Department with the insights needed to create exceptional work.

After introducing the concept to C/D/M, Jane Newman, an account planner, became head of their New York office.

Tom McElligott chose a former C/D/M account planner, Rob White, as one of the partners at his new advertising agency, McElligott Wright Morrison White.

At other agencies, account planning is known by many other names, such as Consumer Insight and Strategic Planning. At the root is a commitment to understanding the consumer and explaining the consumer to other members of the agency team.

The Account Planning function, and its variants, have changed the way agencies develop advertising.

It's impact has been truly revolutionary.

A Brief History

To understand how Account Planning began, it's helpful to understand the British advertising business in the late 60s and early 70s.

The nature of the British advertising business, with less reliance on more expensive quantitative research, more use of qualitative data from smaller samples and fewer layers of client approval, made the environment more receptive to this change in approach.

At the time, there were also numerous smaller agencies breaking away from larger British firms and these new agencies needed to organize more efficiently (a large research department was a luxury few could afford).

One example was BMP (Boase Massimi Pollitt), a small agency which included a former Cambridge boxer turned media director named Stanley Pollitt.

In 1965, Pollitt introduced the *concept* of planning when he was at Pritchard Wood & Partners. "The agency researcher," he said, "was to act as 'The Account Man's conscience.'"

"He was charged with ensuring that all the data relevant to key advertising decisions should be properly analyzed, complemented with new research, and brought to bear on judgements of the creative strategy and how the campaign should be appraised."

It was the first formal attempt to integrate people directly responsible for understanding consumers into what had been a very intuitive process of creating advertising in Britain.

The result? Disaster! Pollitt had identified the need, but picked the wrong people for the job. Still a common problem. But the idea itself began to catch on. Other agencies tried to work with the concept.

Some of the first agencies to develop this function were Collett Dickerson Pearce and the London office of J.Walter Thompson, which re-named their Marketing Department the Account Planning Department in 1967.

In 1968, Pollitt joined with two partners and formed Boase Massini Pollitt (BMP) and planning was made an integral component of the agency's philosophy and practice. They were the first "new breed" planning agency with as many account planners as there were account executives.

This significant change in the way accounts were handled was also the result of a number of other pressures that were occuring at about the same time.

Other Causes of "The Revolution"

During this period, British clients were becoming more marketing conscious and more interested in the purchasing habits of their consumers.

Agency "Marketing" departments began to suffer from redundancy as, more and more, account executives and clients thought of themselves as marketers. There was in-creasing reluctance to defer to people with a similar title.

Client Marketing departments were developing their own quantitative research functions, which made many agency services in this area increasingly redundant. More impor-tantly, there was increasing reluctance to use or pay for these "extra" services.

Yet, there were many functions that remained both necessary and helpful, particularly a concern with information
from the marketplace.

Agencies realized that there was a real need to retain
specialists skilled in the handling of information about the
consumer and the marketplace.

In some ways, it was becoming even more important, with
ever greater amounts of information being generated, and
client decision-making becoming more layered and complex.

Meanwhile, there was great discontent with the way research was used as part of the advertising process.

In many agency operations, the research function was often
used quite late; testing developed advertising as opposed to
using research as a part of the development of advertising.

Certainly this is something many researchers have advo-
cated for years– and the advertising business has many
examples where early insights provided by research have
been responsible for the creation of effective advertising.

But there were all too many examples of research being
used as a "win/lose" decision tool in testing developed
advertising. Usually this was testing of storyboards or rough
"animatic" commercials.

Research was used as a provider of early input. The initial
focus group was commonly used, but the process usually
came to a halt at that point.

This misuse of research is a constant source of friction,
particularly with creative departments. As creatives became
more key in British agency management, this point of view
became, not surprisingly, a management point of view.

Tom Luke, account planner at Campbell-Mithun-Esty
notes, "Planners will continue for some time to cope with

creative directors who carry their 'bad research' experiences with them."

"Many researchers have no idea of how disgusted and vindictive a young copywriter or art director can be when their ad is shot down with questionable research.

"When that young creative person eventually becomes head of a creative group or agency, they make their attitudes known and sometimes law."

"Keep the researchers at bay," is a cry oft' heard at many creative shops. But when a creative person trusts that research is supportive and nurturing of great creative advertising, they can then begin to see the benefit of a relationship with a planner.

Needless to say, the most successful account planners have been those who could handle these conflicts and turn them into relationships.

Finally, there was not only discontent with Research Departments, there was significant discontent within British research departments.

In an effort to be "objective" or "neutral," research departments in British agencies often seemed to retreat to the security of established techniques and standardized norms.

Agency research people were not "advocates," nor were they generally part of the agency team. All too often, they showed up, dumped the bad news on the table, and left the meeting.

This also forced people to focus on research techniques, such as a certain method of storyboard testing, rather than the specific task at hand, which might lend itself to a more useful approach to understanding the consumer.

Instead of transmitting useful information to the agency Creative Department, which was now being forced to worry about questionable research scores on storyboard testing, they were kept apart until it was time to tell the creatives whether they had "won" or "lost."

And, since many clients paid for copy testing, but little else, if one was in research and did not have a storyboard to test, well, there often wasn't much that one could do - a frustrating situation.

Researchers knew there were many things that could be done if they were released from the statistical straitjacket of copy testing and allowed to roll up their sleeves and really understand the consumer.

Yet the focus of research became technique rather than what was done with the information. There were data and information, often in abundance, but seldom insight or inspiration.

This was aggravated by the fact that many of the important meetings went on without the research person in attendance. They were brought in and out of problems according to whether there was a problem or a research budget.

So it is perhaps not surprising that many researchers did not relish the role they were relegated to— and much of the push for account planning came from within the ranks of the agency research department.

Each of these circumstances was a powerful force contributing to "The Account Planner" concept:

- Changing client needs.

- Changing use of the marketing function.

- Changing creative/agency management point of view.

- Discontent within the research department.

The result was truly a revolution.

164

Early Controversy & Early Success

As mentioned, account planning began at JWT/London, where it was an outgrowth of the marketing department and at BMP, where it developed out of the media department, primarily because Stanley Pollitt was BMP's media director.

BMP enjoyed great success, and that success reinforced the trend. Planners themselves promoted this "new way" of doing advertising as well.

In 1978, The Account Planning Group was formed "to support and promote the account planning function within advertising agencies." Though this came after the fact.

By the mid 1970s, account planning was a well-accepted function in British agencies and was in the process of being adopted by a small West Coast agency named Chiat/Day.

It was, however, not accepted without some degree of controversy. In addition to a reluctance on the part of agencies to add another decision-maker, there were "schools" of thought on the matter.

At BMP, the planners were involved closely in the development of creative ideas, as well as strategy and campaign appraisal. One of the planner's jobs was to extract "an early indication of consumer response."

Collett's (Collett Dickerson Pearce) had an equally well-articulated philosophy, with the planner functioning as a strategist rather than a researcher, and kept somewhat at arm's distance from the creative.

At JWT, the account representative coordinated the planning group and used planners to set both campaign and *media* objectives. There was also ongoing measurement of how the work was performing in the marketplace.

It has been noted with some amusement that JWT, in those days, had a particularly well-dressed and well-bred group of account people. They just weren't much good at *thinking*. JWT literally hired some people to do the thinking, though they were not well-dressed enough to send to "JWT's rather elegant clients" of the era.

This additional use of planners has since caused much confusion and consternation among U. S. agencies.

As Rob White said in a 4A's paper, *Planning and its Relationship with Account Management*, "This close working relationship should not be confused with interchangeable roles. There is, and must be, a clear delineation of responsibilities between planner and AE."

Where you draw that line depends on the specific agency operational philosophy– or, in a few isolated cases, the relative IQ of those involved.

Here are a few definitions.

This one is attributed to the late Stanley Pollitt of BMP. *"The account planner is that member of the agency's team who is the expert, through background, training, experience and attitudes, <u>at working with information and getting it used</u>- not just marketing research but all the information available to help solve a client's advertising problems."*

Another definition. *"Simply put, account planning serves to channel the <u>consumer's viewpoint</u> to the agency's creative staff <u>during the entire process</u> of making an ad campaign."*

And here's ours. *"Planners are <u>involved</u> and <u>integrated</u> in the creation of marketing strategy and ads. Their <u>responsibility</u> is to bring the consumer to the forefront of the process and to <u>inspire</u> the team to work with the consumer in mind. The planner has a <u>point of view</u> about the consumer and is not shy about expressing it."*

While each definition expresses the idea somewhat differently, you'll notice some common threads.

1. The account planner is well versed in *data* and *information* of all types.

2. The product of the planner's work is *insight* into the consumer.

3. The planner's responsibility to the rest of the agency team is to *inspire* their work with those insights.

Data, information, insight and inspiration - the steps we've tried to familiarize you with throughout this book. These steps also help define the role of the account planner.

Finally, it should be noted that not everyone could be a Planner– at least not a good one. Just as Pollitt's first experiment ended in disaster, many were not up to it. Education and training became continuing concerns.

And, as U.S. agencies were to discover in the 80s, just "bolting on" a bit of planning didn't work. It had to be *integrated* into the process. Not every agency was equipped to make that big a change in the way they did business.

But one U.S. agency was most definitely able to make it work - Chiat/Day, now Chiat/Day/Mojo. Jay Chiat wanted to make his agency special and he viewed account planning as key to achieving that goal.

He felt that planning was crucial to British creative work, which, he believed at the time, was superior to most American advertising. Chiat also most certainly had a point of view on traditional research. He said, *"Research is ancient history, it's archeological. It's what already has been done."*

Planning, on the other hand, is about discovering and inspiring something new. Chiat's commitment to Planning was a major reason why it worked at Chiat/Day. As one person said, "Jay Chiat did not decide to experiment with account planning. He decided to *have* account planning." It is viewed as a key factor in Chiat/Day becoming one of the most successful agencies of the 1980s.

The Account Planner at Chiat/Day

Here's what Chiat/Day thinks about account planning.

• It is a means of achieving superior creative work that is based on sound marketing and relevant strategic thinking.

• It is a means of ascertaining the effectiveness of the particular advertising in the marketplace, and applying the lessons learned.

• It is based on three fundamentals.

A. That to work, advertising must first be noticed.

B. To work, advertising must deeply understand, empathize with and speak the same language as the consumer.

C. That leading edge advertising must be on the leading edge of social change.

Chiat/Day/Mojo believes these fundamentals can be achieved only through direct contact with the target consumer, via the account planner.

And here is how they define the Planner's role.

1. Planners cover the traditional full service agency research function. In addition, planners personally conduct ongoing qualitative research which gives both the agency and the client continuous and invaluable insight into the mindset of the consumer.

2. Planners are marketers. In addition to research skills, the Planner has marketing expertise which allows him/her to understand the implications of the consumer mindset for the whole marketing mix.

168

3. Planners are line managers. This is an important point. They are accountable, particularly in relation to the effectiveness of the advertising.

At C/D/M, account planning is not a staff or service function where people come and go as needed. Planners are involved all the time, working in tandem with both account management and creative.

It involves research-trained people in the process of making ads more fully than the traditional "staff" structure. It also forces them to take more responsibility for the final work.

4. The planner's principal "product" is The Creative Brief. "The Creative Brief" is a term used more often at British agencies. Basically, it is a document that "briefs" the creative department on the particular advertising problems at hand. But a good creative brief is more than that.

At its best, it is a carefully constructed document aimed at focusing the creative department on a consumer message that is relevant and motivating. It provides the creative department with vital Consumer Insight.

A Few Examples

Here's how account planning and Consumer Insights helped make effective advertising at Chiat/Day for Bazooka Bubble Gum. Planners discovered that kids perceived Bazooka as old-fashioned because it wasn't soft.

This new insight aided the creative staff in developing the campaign theme, *"Are you tough enough for the hard stuff?"*

Said Chiat, "Through account planning, we've taken a perceived defect and turned it into a benefit."

The work of account planners has also contributed to the visibility and success of many of C/D/M's other accounts - from Pizza Hut to Eveready to Nissan Motors.

169

Here's how Dave Ropes, who was head of marketing for Pizza Hut when it was at Chiat/Day, described it:

"The planner is like having your heavy user in the strategic and creative meetings.

"You have a guy sitting across from you being your target, emulating how the heavy user would react to something. What we're talking about is an on-line agency research source, rather than a staff research function that comes in and out only on a problem and doesn't totally understand your business."

Additional Controversy

Research vs. Account Planning vs. Account Service

One of the thorniest issues in making account planning work in American agencies has been distinguishing it from traditional agency research.

Traditional agency researchers and account planners seem to have had the most difficulty understanding each other. While account planners must be versed in and capable of working with every research tool and source of information, account planners have tended to emphasize direct conversations with consumers over impersonal survey results.

Thus, account planners have been charged with a lack of rigor and discipline and with over-relying on their individual intuition to develop consumer insights.

In many cases, the sides have squared off - "qualitative" account planners on the one hand and "quantitative" researchers on the other - neither willing to budge.

But the true difference between planners and researchers has more to do with the role they play in the development of advertising than with the tools they rely on.

1.) Account planning is a fundamental and creative part of ad development - an integral part of the agency team.

2.) As such, it is involved on a continuous basis with an account - very much in harness with account management, creatives and the client.

3.) Account planning is particularly important in creative development *before* the creative team ever puts pen to paper. The account planner is involved in the development of strategy and the creative brief where, after all, the information available to creatives is so much more useful and reliable, and much less inhibiting, than it is at the later execution pre-testing stage.

4.) The account planner is, unapologetically, a person with a point of view- not hiding behind the objective "voice of a thousand households," but with an outlook developed from all the data, of course, but also from his or her own experience and views about advertising. The planner is someone who can inject stimuli and stimulation into the creative process. The planner is an "advocate."

5.) Importantly, the planner is someone who does not leave the meeting after the information is presented, and is actively committed to translating the data and information into actionable insights and inspirations.

Many traditional agency researchers would argue that this is, in fact, the role they have always taken. In Joe Plummer's words, account planning is just "research done right." And, in many cases, this is true.

But, all too often, researchers have remained detached and dispassionate, either feeling discouraged from that role or feeling that their own demands for objectivity prohibit them from "getting so involved."

Learning to Make Account Planning Work

Because account planning represents such a strong shift in the way advertising is developed at most U.S. agencies, it's a role that is often difficult to incorporate in an existing agency.

Realistically, most large agencies don't have the luxury of starting up fresh with a planner as a partner the way Tom McElligott began with Rob White when they started McElligott Wright Morrison White.

There is also a view that there is something "uniquely British" about account planning. As a result, U.S. implementation of it has been quite spotty.

Dave Berger, former Director of Research at FCB, notes that, when asked to describe the "moment of insight," it consistently emerged as part of an internal debate in which the Planner participated.

Berger notes that this tradition of debate is uniquely British and extends even to Parliament, where the Prime Minister must debate members of the opposition as a matter of course.

American traditions, meanwhile, are more bureaucratic and hierarchical. The friction of free-flowing debate, while it certainly happens within agencies, is often subordinated to other organizational concerns. So, someone whose job it is to bring an argument into the meeting is not apt to be penciled into the organization chart at American agencies.

As planner Rob White noted, after an unsuccessful period at a major advertising agency, *They wanted planning, but they didn't want the consequences of planning. You don't rock the boat in client service, where layers and layers of management say you can't do something because it's been done another way for 30 years.*

Different Definitions, Different Titles

There are many differences in the way agencies are organized and many differences in titles and job descriptions - often different titles for identical functions and identical titles for functions that may vary greatly between agencies.

For this, and other reasons, account planning now has many different titles and many different definitions. In fact, some of the following information is sure be out of date as you read this.

Many agencies have reorganized and refocused their research departments, adding the planning function. Some agencies call it "consumer" or "strategic" planning.

Since account planning developed as part of relatively new agency structures, established agencies who wished to add or even test the function had to reorganize, usually a painful and risky process. It was often more efficient and less risky to reorganize at the next level down, at the account level.

This could also be implemented gradually, account by account, learning as one goes.

Often, the planner is a member of an agency account team which includes an account executive and a creative group.

In general, each account has its own team and its own account planner. On smaller accounts, the planner may have numerous account responsibilities, similar to other members of agency management.

Here are some examples of agency terminology related to account planning: Wells, Rich, Greene calls its planners *marketing directors*. NW Ayer has *AyerPlan*. J. Walter Thompson/West has *Strategic Planning Directors*.

BBDO/LA gives the Research Director planning responsibilities using a "team" structure. At DMB&B, the planners report directly to the Creative Director. They have found good planners from fields as diverse as Art History, Anthropology and Dream Research.

A related development at British agencies (with a few examples in the U.S.) is the growth of "Brand Groups," which broadens the Agency Team concept (account executive, account planner and creative group) to include a media manager, and, sometimes, the client.

The agency team is also similar to the organization of many student agency groups: "Campaigns" classes, student agencies and ad competitions, such as the AAF/NSAC Contest.

So, if you're a new agency, or a student agency with few research resources, you may have a few advantages in making account planning work for you.

But whatever it's called, it generally represents an active shift from providing information and being a "score-keeper" to providing Consumer Insight and becoming an active part of the development of the advertising itself.

The Future of Account Planning

As the account planning function becomes more common, we will surely have ample examples of "bad account planning" to put things into better perspective.

Chuck Overholser of BJK&E described the two possible extremes of the contributions of planners:

"When she is good, she contributes a deeper, more insightful understanding of consumers and how they react to stimuli. She tells how the market really works in flesh and blood terms, and relates this information to the market problem. The planner, unlike the traditional researcher, is an invaluable personal intermediary between consumers and creatives– the catalyst between information and the creative world. The result is advertising which enthralls the consumer, creates a sympathetic closeness to the product and makes people want to buy."

174

On the other hand...

"When she (or he) is bad, she uses suspect, invalid data which she manipulates and controls. She gains the trust of creative people by helping them get ideas and selling their favorites. She's not trained in traditional survey research methods and thus may lose sight of the benefits that are important to the brand's target segments. She makes very little use of experimental methods to test advertising for clarity of communication or power to shift beliefs and attitudes about the brand. The result is advertising which, although entertaining, is often ineffective in the marketplace."

There will be a wider range of examples in the U.S. as more and more agencies and marketers use a more active search for Consumer Insight as part of the advertising process.

In this context, we can be certain that the account planning process will become an increasingly important part of the way agencies make advertising.

Equally certain is that, for the most part, it won't be called account planning.

"Planning" is a confusing descriptor. Many people, at both the client and the agency, are involved in some sort of planning. The exclusive use of this word attached to one person's job is confusing at best, and offensive at worst.

The word "account" is less limiting, but it has been used by account service in the same way that media, creative and research have been used by their respective departments.

Finally, more and more agency people in every agency function will find themselves working for and searching for consumer insights as part of their job. As Gabe Massimi, Stanley Pollitt's partner, said, *"Leo Burnett was a great planner by instinct."* So are many of the best and brightest minds in advertising.

In every job, as marketing and advertising demand greater insights to gain competitive advantage in the marketplace, the search for Consumer Insight will grow from a new job called account planning to a major reworking of the way we develop advertising. And we will need people trained in the discovery and expression of Consumer Insight.

Call it account planning, call it "research done right," whatever it's called tomorrow, it all drives toward the discovery of Consumer Insight. And in the future, to some extent, all of us will become account planners.

19 THE ROLE OF THE ACCOUNT PLANNER

In this chapter, we want to describe the account planner's job in more detail. So you can get a feel for what it might be like to be one.

The account planner is primarily *an insight manager*, first accumulating and analyzing consumer and market information, distilling the insights and then communicating those insights to the rest of the account team, usually in the form of "The Creative Brief."

While the job is ongoing and interactive, the planner has specific roles during each stage of campaign development.

These are the 5 basic stages:

1. Discovering and Defining the Advertising Task.

2. Preparing the Creative Brief.

3. Creative Development.

4. Presenting the Advertising to the Client.

5. Track the Advertising's Performance.

First, we will summarize each of the five stages, and then cover them in more detail.

1. Discovering and Defining the Advertising Task

The account planner organizes information about the consumer and the marketplace from every source available: from existing client and ad agency research to secondary research and sales data, to primary research organized by the planner.

(Some of this research may be like the "Consumer Excursion" we talked about earlier.)

First and foremost, a good account planner must be a curious person. The purpose of this curiosity is to discover the job of advertising for this product in this segment of the market.

2. Preparing The Creative Brief

The account planner prepares the creative brief, which presents the key insights to the Creative Department, client and account management.

But the core function of this document is to "brief" the Creative Department on the consumer and *inspire* the team to the task at hand.

The creative brief focuses on the issues pertinent to the development of the advertising from the consumer's point of view and presents other important marketing aspects of the product category.

It also helps to define the proper positioning of the brand in a way that embodies both its rational and emotional aspects.

3. Creative Development

During the development of the advertising, the account planner represents the consumer's point-of-view (is the consumer advocate we spoke of) within the agency.

The account planner interacts with all members of the agency, but primarily with the Creative Department.

Sometimes the planner discusses possible consumer reactions to various advertising approaches, or represents the consumer's mindset in development meetings.

Other times, the planner actually gets consumer reaction to early advertising concepts.

BMP, the first British agency formed by a planner, had a

high level of commitment in this regard. Here's how it was described by Stanley Pollitt. *"All creative work- and we mean all creative work - at BMP is checked out qualitatively with a tightly-defined target market.*

"Commercials are checked out in rough animatic form, typically with four discussion groups of about eight respondents each; press advertisements are checked out in individual depth interviews with some 20 respondents. Target market samples are recruited by our own network of 80 recruiters, the majority of these outside London. Account planners are the moderators of the groups or depths.

"To give some idea of scale, we conducted some 1,200 groups last year, which arguably makes us the largest qualitative research company in the country."

In account planning, the key is insightful input as early as possible in the creative process, presented in such a way as to stimulate the best possible work from the creative department. This input is usually *qualitative* - based on small sample research and judgment and usually occurs much earlier than in many traditional agency research settings, where close to final executions are subjected to win/lose types of research far along in their development.

4. Presenting the Advertising to the Client

The account planner can also help *sell* the advertising. For example, the Account Planner helps sell ads by explaining exactly how they work with the consumer.

This is rooted in one of the key advantages the account planner has in the client/agency structure:

The client says, *"This is my product."*

The account executive says, *"This is my client."*

The Creative Director says, *"This is my ad."*

The account planner says, *"This is my consumer."*

The account planner represents the consumer's point-of-view during the presentation to the client.

The account planner's consumer orientation is a powerful platform for selling a piece of consumer persuasion, i.e. "Here's how and why the consumer will react to this advertising."

From this platform, the planner can articulate how the ad or campaign will work in the marketplace and, in so doing, reassure the client about the advertising decisions.

This can also help defend against erosion and compromise by maintaining focus on the consumer's reaction to the advertising (rather than the agency's or client's).

5. Track the Advertising's Performance

The account planner tracks reaction to the advertising in the marketplace, providing additional information to the creative and account groups. The account planner plays a key part in managing an ongoing relationship with the consumer, exploring and developing further evolutions of the advertising program or campaign.

The account planner continually asks the question, "Do they get it?" and "What does it mean to them?" And reports back to the agency team.

This input is key to subsequent executions and extensions of the advertising campaign.

Many times this is accomplished with large-scale, highly controlled "tracking studies." Other times, the planner continues his or her on-going dialogue with the consumer to get his reactions to the brand and the advertising.

The Account Planner's Job

Now let's take a deeper look at the account planner's job at each stage of the development process.

1. Defining the Advertising Task

The planner's job begins with working to understand the market, the brand and, most of all, the consumer - who that consumer is and how to motivate him or her.

Here are the major types of activities at this early stage of the development process.

• Analysis of Current Marketing Information

Trying to collect and absorb as much data as possible about the client and competitors, the account planner combines the technical data and intellectual discipline of studying marketing information with the deductive reasoning and intuition that comes from conversations with consumers.

• Conversations with Consumers

During this stage of the process, the planner works to put a human face on this data for the account and creative members of the agency team. And, the goal is to find the Sweet Spot.

Account Planners have tended to emphasize one on one interviews and focus groups. The planner may use a variety of the techniques that we discussed earlier in the book.

These consumer conversations may cover areas such as language and feelings related to brands in the category, usage patterns, and reactions to current advertising. The planner works to mesh insights into the consumer and the category with insights into the brand.

• Debate and Discussion with Agency and Client Personnel

During the entire process of investigation and discovery,

the planner works with other members of the agency team.

For example, during the development of the IBM System/400 advertising, the client and agency began with the belief that they should emphasize the power of the computer.

Planning discovered that,while power was important, consumers were more concerned about whether the equipment could grow with their business.

• Defining the Advertising Task

This activity drives toward defining the ultimate task of the advertising.

The shape of the solution is a result of how one defines the problem to be solved– the advertising task. It's not always as simple as it sounds.

The responsibility for this will vary from agency to agency. In British operations, account planners have had more impact on the definition of the advertising task or the positioning statement than in U.S. ad agencies where, traditionally, many people have played an important role - from the client to the Creative Director.

Regardless of division of responsibility, the task must be defined and the planner must have a major involvement and, in many cases, primary responsibility.

Here is a classic example of the definition of the advertising task based on a consumer insight.

Example- Defining the Task for Band-Aid™

As you no doubt know, Johnson & Johnson's Band-Aid brand has a dominant market share in the bandage market.

Primary usage is by young children. And mothers of young children are the primary purchasers.

Most keep the product in the bathroom medicine cabinet.

They are familiar with the product, use the product when the child has a minor injury, and have a positive attitude toward the product and manufacturer.

What should the task for the advertising be?

Answer- The Advertising Task for Band-Aid™

After much examination of the market, Young & Rubicam, Johnson & Johnson's advertising agency, discovered an insight which revealed an opportunity for Band-Aid brand bandages and helped define the task for the advertising.

They discovered that there was indeed an opportunity for increased usage of Band-Aid brand bandages. They discovered that after a scab formed, the Band-Aid was quite often not replaced.

They also discovered that the scab was often knocked off or the cut re-opened and, as a result, healing took longer and the child was exposed to the risk of additional infection.

Since mothers already had the product, they merely had to be informed in a dramatic and persuasive way that they could protect their young child's welfare by using a fresh Band-Aid after the first one was removed.

This was the task for the advertising: to inform mothers of young children that they should keep a fresh bandage on their child's cut longer to insure proper protection and promote better healing.

After the task is defined, usually based on a Consumer Insight, it becomes time to prepare the Creative Brief.

2. Preparing The Creative Brief

In general, a good Creative Brief addresses these key issues:

• Who is the Typical Target Consumer?

In terms of demographics.

In terms of psychographics.

In terms of usage and behavior.

• How Do Consumers View the Brand?

• What is the Role for Advertising?

How well these key issues are answered is the key to developing a good creative brief.

There are many ways to write this document. But however it's written, it should *focus on the consumer.* It should be written from his or her viewpoint and should use his or her terminology.

This document introduces the creative department to the person they're talking to.

Good creative briefs and good account planners seem to have a sort of knack for helping a creative department "get off on the right foot." As Joe Plummer of DMB&B says, *"A good account planner knows how to teach people how to see things."*

Here is a good view of how to develop a good creative brief, from FCB/London.

A. Get to Know Your Creative Team.

In many ways, one of the key jobs of the account planner is to get to know and win the confidence of the creative team. This is necessary to develop the commitment and teamwork required for developing good creative briefs and, in the end, good advertising. Often, getting the creative team to hit the consumer's Sweet Spot means you have to hit theirs first.

B. The Brief Must be Single-Minded.

Though it's not always possible, FCB London aims for one single sentence that sums up the desired consumer response.

A hodgepodge of consumer responses won't be helpful when the advertising effort must be focused.

Even a very clearcut and single-minded brief can still generate many creative thoughts and ideas.

C. The Brief Should Contain an Imaginative Description of the Target Group.

Again, the account planner's job is to play consumer advocate– to represent the consumer. A well-crafted presentation of who that consumer is, how they feel and behave, is vital for helping the creative, account and client personnel understand to whom they're selling. Sometimes conceptual models are used.

The account planner puts the consumer at the table with all the other members of the team.

An imaginative description opens the door to insight. It helps the creative group more clearly visualize the consumer's Sweet spot.

D. The Brief Should be Brand Specific.

This could be rooted in the physical aspects of the product, or related to emotions and imagery. Hopefully, the Brief will provide a distinctive insight into the brand that could be no one else's.

A good Consumer Insight will *link* an insight about the consumer with an insight about the brand.

For example, in the development of the Energizer Pink Bunny campaign, Planners helped the agency arrive at the insight that Energizer could not avoid challenging DuraCell's long-lasting position, but, rather, had to out-execute the competition and build an engaging brand personality based on the identical long-lasting position.

3. Creative Development

During the actual development of advertising, the planner is always available to answer questions, hear ideas in their early stages and to encourage the creatives to stay focused on the consumer.

This is a delicate task. The planner must be encouraging without leading and directive without being dictatorial.

A planner's success at this stage depends a great deal on his or her judgment and on the strong, trusting relationships which have been built with the creative department.

4. Presenting the Advertising to The Client

The account planner is in a unique position to *sell* the work.

The client says, *"This is my product."*

The account executive says, *"This is my client."*

The Creative Director says, *"This is my ad."*

The account planner says, *"This is my consumer."*

Often, the account planner participates in the actual presentation of the work.

The account planner can play a role at two or three specific places in the presentation.

A. During the Introductory Section.

It is usually the account planner's job to present a brief version of the creative brief, setting the stage for the advertising to follow.

Sometimes this information is contained in someone else's piece of the presentation. For example, in a condensed presentation to senior client management, this information might be contained in some remarks by senior agency management.

But the focus on the consumer is an important part of the introduction, and is often done by the account planner.

B. Presentation of the "Key Insight."

Sometimes this presentation can be quite elaborate, including videotapes of consumers or other methods for bringing new consumer concepts to life.

C. How the Consumer Reacts to the Advertising.

Whether as a formal part of the presentation, or as part of general discussion, this is a key contribution of the agency's account planner.

It serves to remind client and agency alike that the advertising which is being discussed is not for the agency or for the client, but, rather, for the consumer.

5. The Feedback Stage– Tracking the Advertising

Here is another important job for the account planner.

After the advertising is produced and the client tracks his sales, and the account executive tracks billings and the creatives, perhaps, hope for some advertising awards, the account planner works to discover if the advertising is working with the consumer.

Do they get it? What do they get? What do they remember?

Are there any dynamics in the marketplace that can or should impact on the next stage of the advertising?

What's going on? What's new?

The account planner keeps asking questions and works to bring back new answers and new information to the agency.

Over the long-haul, this is an invaluable contribution, as it maximizes the effect of the advertising in the marketplace and maximizes the effect of the consumer on the advertising.

The cumulative impact of advertising builds brands.

The account planner helps to manage this vital brand-building function and make both his client's advertising and his agency stronger.

This unique understanding of how advertising works in the mind of the consumer has played a major role in Chiat/Day treating many of their major advertising campaigns as "events."

It is an example of account planning helping to develop insights that impact the entire operation of the agency.

And that's the role of the account planner from start to finish.

Over the last decade, account planning has revolutionized the advertising process in the country of its birth, and, in the U.S., it has become an important part of the renewed recognition of the importance of Consumer Insight.

What Makes for a Good Account Planner

You may find yourself interested in doing something related to account planning.

Remember, account planning is an approach, rather than a "system" to be applied identically across all accounts. And, as we said, the role is different from agency to agency.

But whatever you call it, it needs to be constantly worked at to be done correctly.

Therefore, intelligence, experience, strong observational skills and, most of all, judgement, are key characteristics for successful account planners.

Interpersonal skills are important.

It involves relationship management as insight management. planners foster collaboration among all members of the agency team and between the agency and the client.

At the same time, an account planner must be good at developing, maintaining and communicating his or her own point of view, that is, the consumer's point-of-view. Getting along with your team while neglecting the consumer's point of view is most certainly an example of "bad account planning."

A good account planner must be thoughtful and careful with information.

As Pollitt said, *"The planner's job is the continuous analysis and interpretation of the available information: its assessment, both its uses and, as crucially, maybe more crucially, its limitations. To move the data forward, give it dynamism, to provide illumination, bring it alive. Condense it for everyone else involved."*

Finally, a good planner must be someone who is passionate about advertising.

If you decide on a career in this exciting field, we wish you well on what is sure to be an exciting career.

And, if you do become an account planner, we hope you become a good one. People who provide consumer insight are vital to the industry.

We will never have enough of them.

20 INSIGHTS ON THE FIRING LINE

by Karen Randolph
Sr. vp, Director, Consumer Resources
Foote, Cone & Belding/Chicago

James Playsted Wood in his landmark textbook, "_The Story of Advertising_," said of research:

"(An) attempt to apply scientific method to advertising...(aimed) at mechanizing what has long been practiced as craft...(It) has taken much of the color and life out of modern advertising. (It) does not often produce ideas..."

That, in a nutshell, was how research in an advertising agency used to work. The traditional view of researchers conjured up images of "number crunchers" who sit off in darkened corners, wear green eye shades and prepare memos that outline in a detached, detailed manner the scores agency advertising has received from a copy testing procedure.

Not at Foote, Cone & Belding. We've redefined the role of agency research. Redefined it to truly leverage, for the agency, the talent, knowledge and life experience that resides within our department. In fact, we've even changed the department's name to Consumer Resources to reflect our pro-active role.

There are three facets to this redefinition, but at its core is _our focus on the consumer._ We call it "consumer immersion." We have made it our job to know more about the brands our clients have entrusted to us– and better understand the consumers of those brands– than anyone else inside or outside the agency.

190

It is up to us, Consumer Resources professionals, to uncover insights about these prospects that will stimulate or inspire or spark the creative people and the creative process. We have no crystal ball, and we harbor no illusions that the "big idea" will come from us. But, we've made it our job to drive the creative process, to feed it and nurture it through consumer understanding, rather than drain "the color and life out of it."

To accomplish this, we ensure that our Consumer Resources people receive training in the traditional methods of research. Then we insist that they move beyond these. Research is merely one of the tools available to us. We have broadened our definition of what constitutes "data," of what is useful information, to include thoughts, hypotheses and insights that accrue from observational, ethnographic and other non-traditional methods.

We mobilize every resource at hand...psychology, sociology, pop culture, new trends and synthesize all this data to reach for the essence of the consumer's mind, heart and soul...epiphanies that can ignite creative momentum.We have become quite successful in getting this information accepted as valid and salient, not only by agency personnel, but also by our partners on the client side.

A second aspect of the redefinition of our role concerns the *transformation of the researcher from "unbiased observer" to "consumer advocate"* in the strategic and creative development processes. We believe strongly that it is not enough to immerse yourself in the consumer. Once you've devoted years of experience to understanding him, you have to ensure that his voice is heard– his point-of-view represented– when we're formulating our strategies and our advertising.

A writer once said, "To die for an idea is to set a rather high price on conjecture." While we don't recommend suicide, we fight with all our might for our beliefs.

A third part of the redefinition of the role of research within the agency has to do with personal responsibility. We have always espoused, and have now won acceptance throughout the ranks, that *Consumer Resources professionals must take responsibility for the advertising produced on their accounts.* No more darkened corners or places to hide. The first outward sign we had accomplished this was when the people of our department began lovingly amassing their own creative "reels." They started portfolios of the advertising they contributed to; work they helped create.

Consumer Resources professionals have changed their mind-set. They think of themselves as advertising people first, researchers second. Everything they do is single-mindedly focused on how they can help improve their product...which is *advertising,* not research. In other words, they understand that their primary purpose is as a catalyst to help the agency do better creative work. They let this mandate guide what they do and how they do it.

Breakthrough creative solutions can come from any department. They begin with a keen intuition, a passion for communication and a deep personal involvement with the brand. Beyond those attributes, a researcher must possess an ability to think strategically, coupled with an enthusiasm for delving into the consumer's psyche and articulating what has been learned about his relationship with the brand. And finally, the researcher must possess skills to effectively present the relevance of the advertising's strategic solution to the consumer.

This is a drastically different orientation than the traditional role of research. But it is one which we believe has resulted in more successful advertising being developed...ads that unleash new sales energy in the marketplace for our clients.

Some examples are in order. Canada Dry Ginger Ale had a strong image of being a high-quality product for adults. But traditional and non-traditional research told us that many consumers perceived the brand as a drink for older adults. In fact, some consumers equated it with their grandparents' generation.

Our analysis of America's baby boomers revealed that they have steadfastly retained their youthful love of soft drinks into middle age. They have decreased their coffee and alcohol consumption. They are searching for a "good for you" alternative that's clean, light, dry and not "kid-sweet."

These insights led us to marry the problem– the perception of the brand as an older person's drink– to the opportunity– a large untapped market of boomers.

Synthesizing psychographic and demographic research, we positioned Canada Dry as the ideal beverage for boomers who will not yield their youthful self-attitudes. The adult soft drink, one better suited to many occasions than alcoholic beverages.

Our brand personality statement said, "Canada Dry embodies a fun, youthful attitude toward adulthood with a relentless spirit that refuses to age in a traditional way."

Television commercials featured an updated high-energy, gospel version of the old ballad "Young at Heart." They pictured active, young adults at work and at leisure living life to the fullest, with a slight bow to their maturity. They tagline became: "Always light, always dry, always 'Young at Heart,' Canada Dry Ginger Ale." The campaign has succeeded in repositioning Canada Dry for a new audience.

Pearle, Inc., the largest eyecare retailer in America, also wanted to tap the boomer market, knowing that ninety percent of the population requires vision correction as they approach middle-age.

Using non-traditional research, we confirmed deeply-held stereotypes that glasses are a visual symbol of advancing age which don't often flatter people's looks.

So once again, we married the problem– the negative perception of glasses– to the opportunity– boomers want to feel attractive, young and fashionable.

Synthesizing psychographic, demographic research as well as fashion trends, we positioned Pearle eyewear as a stylish fashion accessory. Glasses are a vehicle for boomers to express their moods and make a fashion statement at work or play; an extensive eyewear wardrobe captures the boomer's quest for individuality. In order to fuel the demand for multiple pairs of glasses, a "buy one, get one pair free" promotion was incorporated in the advertising.

Television advertising featured video vignettes of attractive, fit people in a myriad of situations from shopping to dining to enjoying a concert on the beach. The hand-held camera technique, coupled with the very contemporary styling of those in eyewear, gave the ads the tone of a hip fashion lay-out. Different film styles from grainy black and white to color captured people in diverse moods. The classic Isley Brothers' 1966 song..."It's Your Thing" energized the spots and appealed to boomers. The tagline was: "Pearle knows there's no excuse for having only one pair of glasses."

The campaign gave Pearle a unique brand personality in a category known for pedestrian retail price ads. It helped boomers realize that stylish eyewear can actually enhance your appearance, and it significantly increased sales.

For Quintessence, Incorporated, the fragrance company, we created a print campaign for Dare, the women's cologne, that departed from the category's traditional reliance on romance and fantasy.

Accomplished women achievers in daring occupations

194

such as auto racing, rock climbing and wildlife photography were depicted on-the-job and in evening clothes. The stark, yet powerful visual images of risk-takers appeared with the fragrance's challenging and intriguing tagline: "Anything is possible if you Dare."

Psychographic research and the impact of the women's movement on society convinced us that women would welcome and appreciate a new archetype of female beauty...a woman whose accomplishments are just as compelling as her physical image.

The consumer response to the campaign was unprecedented in Quintessence's history. The company was innundated with phone calls and mail suggesting other "daring" women for future campaigns. And, to our delight and theirs, sales responded accordingly.

FCB has reaped enormous benefits by encouraging researchers to become true collaborative partners in the advertising development process.

Today, FCB's Consumer Resources Group continues to expand the scope and depth of its research activities in order to serve as the "voice of the consumer" in shaping integrated communications strategies for our clients.

Karen Randolph is Senior Vice President and Director of Consumer Resources at Foote, Cone & Belding/Chicago.

She has served such clients as Cadbury, Schweppes, Citibank, Coors Brewing Co., Kraft General Foods and SC Johnson Wax. In 1989, she became the leader in developing FCB's Consumer Resources Group.

A graduate of Notre Dame, she lectures frequently at DePaul and Loyola universities.

21 INSIGHT IN ACTION

by Robb Bell, Mt. Hood Group

I believe the real challenge for those of us in marketing is translating the lessons and principles in Lisa's book into meaningful and profitable actions.

The principles of Consumer Insight as they relate to Brand Management have been a significant part of seminars I've given over the years to marketing management.

So, after I read Lisa's book, I reviewed my seminar materials and extracted those points that are most relevant to the ones Lisa made and most useful to those in Brand Management.

I'll be serving up a lot of bullet points and a few examples to dramatize where things can go wrong– or, hopefully, where things can go right. Sort of a slide show without the slides.

First, based on my experience, I want to emphasize two basic "truths" that I believe are absolutely critical to a successful career in Brand Management.

1. The most important functional skill of a successful marketing person is understanding and communicating with the consumer and the trade.

There are so many "housekeeping" concerns that come with running a business, that it's easy to assume and then forget this obvious fact. We get so caught up with the details of our businesses, that the human factor, which never shows up on those computer print-outs, can be functionally removed from our day-to-day jobs.

It's up to you to maximize the human dimension of your business and make the real live people you deal with one of your Brand's strategic advantages.

196

Since our focus is the consumer, I'm not going to talk much about Trade relations, but I'll make two related points.

First, I've found that great Sales Managers develop the same kind of encyclopedic and insightful knowledge of their customers that we must develop of our product's consumers. Their knowledge of the trade sets a standard we have to match with our knowledge of the consumer.

Second, even in these days of slotting allowances, the trade knows when their customers want a product. The trade knows and respects a good advertising program- one that connects with the people who show up to shop in their stores. And I've never heard a member of the trade worth doing business with suggest that they wanted you to spend less on advertising your brands.

Certainly, that has often been the result- but it was never the intent. The trade respects brands that know how to talk to their customers.

They continue to respect you even as they hold you upside down to shake loose that extra trade allowance.

Which brings us to the second critical factor related to successful Brand Management.

2. One of the best opportunities we have to make significant contributions to our business is to conceive, execute and test *BIG* ideas.

This almost always involves some sort of advertising. Or, as they often say these days,"integrated marketing communications." Frankly, I've always found that a strong focused advertising program is key to any marketing effort- however integrated it might be.

A meaningful consumer message, whether it shows up in a heavy user direct mail program, or a network TV schedule bulging with GRP's is absolutely critical to your business.

I believe that much of the absolutely heroic effort I have seen, with people striving mightily to manage their way around the lack of this critical element, could have been much more productively used working on that one critical issue– how we communicate to our customers.

Spend your time working to find that one big meaningful idea that, as Lisa says, "Hits the Sweet Spot."

I've seen old "cash cow" brands brought back in from the pasture and revitalized with a new advertising message, and I've seen new business result from focused explorations into "low BDI" areas that had been ignored for years. In each case, that single differentiating factor is effective consumer communication.

With that in mind, I've pulled out a few more slides from a seminar called **"General Areas of Consideration for Business Review,"** (If you want the whole thing, call my office) and I'd like to take you through some critical check-points related to generating insight into your consumer.

First, a few slides from the Strategy Section...

• **Do we know why consumers do/do not use our Brand?** This is a fundamental question you must continue to ask during your stewardship of your brand.

Kraft used to be the standard for "good for you" family food. Now, a growing number of consumers perceive it in a dramatically different way. Generations and their attitudes change over time. Today, more quickly than ever. Attitudes from a few years ago may be out of date.

Here are some of the important related points.

• **What are the important factors in a consumer's purchase decision?**

• **How does our promotion/copy satisfy those factors?**

• Are we doing any research to better understand what these factors are?

I'd like to focus on this one a bit– most brands develop a history, a collection of "lore" of what does and doesn't work. And, while some principles remain constant, one of those is that the world keeps changing.

During my early years at P&G, convenience was not seen to be anything you could build a brand on and "Green Marketing" was viewed as a fringe issue. We see how fast things change.

You should be testing to check premises that have been long established as eternal truths on your brand. Next...

• How do consumers perceive our Brand?

Remember, people liking your commercials is not enough. Alka-Seltzer's "That'sa spicy meatball" campaign was fun and famous and won awards. But business fell apart– because while the commercial so vividly displayed the problem, no one bothered to remember the solution.

• What does usage/attitude data say?

For years, S. C. Johnson marketing management focused annual budget discussions on share growth, which was always up. Finally, it was noticed that shipments were down... and the truth came out. Floors that needed wax were disappearing under carpet and no-wax floors.

And some points related to The Working Consumer...

• What is the Brand doing to reach the working consumer?

• How important is the working consumer?

This has been one of my major areas of concern. And I believe it's important for most brands.

If you work for a consumer packaged goods company that's been around for a number of years, chances are, you work for businesses, and products, that were built on serving the needs of traditional homemakers.

Even though we know intellectually that the world has changed, we don't always run our businesses that way. That picture in our minds of the consumer we think we "know" may be a very out-of-date photograph. For example, a growing percentage of consumers don't speak English. 25-30% of all goods purchases are made by males.

Many brands need to be "refreshed" to catch on with a new generation. Heinz Ketchup "refreshed" itself and stemmed Hunts' growth with the then popular "Anticipation" song by Carly Simon.

Another example– have your SKU's really been keeping up with the spread in purchasing? From the demand for smaller sizes with smaller households and fewer people at meal time, to the demand for larger sizes from the increasingly popular Price Clubs.

The right deal with the right SKU can improve your bottom line fast. Welch's just sold Wal-Mart 1 million cases of Welch's Grape Juice (24 to a case) to generate 24 million consumer impressions in a very short window. In the same category, VeryFine has built a beautiful business in vending machines and hotel room bars– where big marketing budgets aren't found. Or necessary.

• **Are there any minority groups particularly attracted to the Brand?**

Here again, the course of our business day does not often put us in touch with some of our most loyal groups of customers. Some of the reasons for that loyalty are quite different and some avenues we may use for communication are also different than we might be using on our main effort.

These groups can deliver exceptionally high brand index rates and they are deserving of attention merely from a business perspective. As heavy users, they can also be a valuable source of insight. More on this later.

In addition, we as business persons, as well as our companies, will be increasingly judged by how well and thoughtfully we address the needs of a wide range of minority groups.

A significant degree of attention to these issues can be both helpful to your brand in the short-term and to your company in the long-term.

• What are we doing to encourage consumption among current users?

It's fine to know our consumers as human beings and understand them– but, after all, our objective is selling more.

So, now that we know them better, how do we get them to use "a bigger cereal bowl?" How do we get them to serve our product more frequently? Or use it more often?

For all the creative honors bestowed upon all of Alka-Seltzer's agencies and all of their advertising over the years, little attention was given to the single visual idea created by Jack Tinker & Partners at the very beginning of the brand's creative Renaissance.

The BIG idea? Drop two tablets into the glass instead of one. Today, we are enjoying the latest "Plop. Plop. Fizz. Fizz." Anyone who wants to take a close hard look at Alka Seltzer's business will see that this simple idea has had a more substantial impact on their business than any of that engaging advertising.

Now some points from the Media Section...

• How might the Brand better reach our target audience and what must we "give up" to better reach our target?

The changing media marketplace offers some of the most exciting opportunities in Brand Management.

With all the debate and discussion on various aspects of that changing marketplace, I'd like to focus on one key point.

Time after time, I've seen the first brand to "figure out" how to talk to their customers in a new way through a new media channel reap substantial positive benefits.

The reason? It's a lesson I learned as a boy walking along the shores of Cazenovia Lake in upstate New York. The first rock makes the biggest splash.

• Are there target opportunities?

Too often, target discussions wander off into arcane statistical considerations. While I applaud and encourage rigor and discipline in these areas, the numbers often hide what I feel is the real advantage in more targetted media efforts.

They offer you an important opportunity to tell a deeper, more focused, more meaningful, and, hopefully, a more *persuasive* story.

If your agency's creative people can develop a more persuasive message that is made more persuasive by the targetted nature of the media vehicle, I'd think seriously about testing it.

Nothing is healthier in a client/agency relationship than getting the whole team focused on improving and testing persuasion.

As a practical matter, this is one of the main benefits to your brand of exploring targetted media opportunites. And naturally, if that targetted program works, you'll be like a duck on a June bug applying those lessons to your major media efforts.

As you search for the best way to talk to your customer and that BIG advertising idea, naturally you'll be involved in refining an "Advertising Strategy."

This is a much simpler and more specific document than your Marketing Strategy. It needs to reflect the basic appeal and the basic reason-why which will permit the simplest, clearest and most effective presentation of the brand's selling story.

Most importantly, it's what you want to say to your customers, not your management. This is still a real problem in many marketing operations.

All too often, and I think Lisa made this point very well in her book, every point-of-view is well-represented, EXCEPT THE CONSUMER.

I have a lot to say on this topic, and frankly more than can fit in this piece- but it is worth emphasizing that this key document *absolutely* must be based on meaningful insight into your consumer and your brand.

Now here are some slides I pulled from our "Advertising Strategy Seminar." Next slide...

• What is the Agency's assessment of strategies (the Brand's and competition's) in the current environment?

Your competition can teach you a lot. They're talking to the consumer, too. Whatever secret and expensive information they may have, you generally know that the very best thinking is represented in their current advertising copy.

One of the best ways to train yourself to become a good judge of your agency's work, is to analyze the competition's.

Lisa's point about being a good Consumer Detective has great relevance here. Competitive reels are easy to collect. Spend some time with your agency examining and discussing advertising in your category as well as related categories.

This can also be a healthy way for you and your agency to develop a dialogue about advertising.

Think about it. Here's an advertising meeting that won't involve sacrificing your Agency Creative Department's latest brainchild on the conference table.

Look for opportunities to talk with your Agency about the best way to communicate with your consumer when you're not holding a copy meeting. These competitive reviews can be a good place to work to establish that rapport.

Here's a slide from the Promotion Section...

• What has been the Brand's trial event experience?

One of the nicest things you can do for a consumer is make it cheap and easy to use your product. And, it's one of the best ways to grab some quick insights along the way.

I've long been a fan of sampling programs– though not always a fan of their per unit costs. And I've found that younger brand persons who really cared about finding ways to get their product into people's hands, tended to have a positive attitude about that brand that carried over to many other aspects of the business.

Finally, I don't think any of us can ignore Frito-Lay's recent activities with SmartFood in this area. I guarantee that anyone who gets a small bag of popcorn handed to them by a six foot bag of popcorn will develop an awareness of that product unmatched by any traditional media message.

Am I recommending that we go out and infest the world with giant versions of our packages? No. Because I also remember that the second rock I threw into Cazenovia Lake didn't make quite the same beautiful splash.

But every brand has to seriously address how they generate trial in the marketplace. Monitoring that trial will provide you with another opportunity for Consumer Insight.

Here's a slide from the Research Section...

• What do we know about the heavy/light brand user?

I've consistently found a comparison between heavy and light users to help focus on the meaningful brand dimensions.

Then, really get to know your heavy user. He or she is a walking, talking Sweet Spot– a gold mine of insight– both about your brand and about your brand's consumers.

The heavy user may know more about your brand than you do. Ask yourself, your agency and your marketing research suppliers these questions:

Who is the heavy user?

Does she (or he) exist?

If so, where does she live?

What is her lifestyle?

How can I communicate with her?

You must understand your consumer– their hopes, and fears, doubts, how many kids they have– anything and everything that is relevant to communicating with them.

Because communicating with your consumer is, as I said at the beginning of this piece, one of the most important functional skills of a successful marketing person.

Finally, I want to talk to you about Market Testing. It's the final place you get acquainted with your consumer. It's "where the rubber meets the road."

Frankly, I believe that a good Brand Manager tries to have a few market tests functioning at all times. Not necessarily big ones, where your reputation and the company's quarterly profits are on the line, but tests just big enough to really learn something.

Not one $6 million test, but three $2 million tests.

Because this is where we as marketers take our game out of the meeting room and put it out there in the marketplace. Sometimes it's a frightening thought. Because it's always a risk, and, as marketers, we're taught to avoid risk.

But I've seen a combination of reluctance to test combined with laboratory tests consistently produce unhappy results.

Two of the most common types:

• Misleading results from "laboratory testing techniques" triggering disasters because of faulty premises.

• Inadequate preparation and an inadequate understanding of key business issues for expansion– tracing to a lack of "real world" testing experience.

There is no substitute for marketplace testing– even if it means letting the competition know what you're up to.

There are ways to accelerate test market reading– to minimize what I have found to be the objectively rare risk of competitive preemption. Accelerating GRP or adding a trial incentive delivery can be done on a very precise basis to gain early insight into repeat rates.

Incidentally, before anyone talks about testing or expansion, *real factory* batch product must be reviewed by real target consumer humans. Factory batch products must also be age-tested with real people, too.

Nothing is worse than a glorious success which quickly rots.

Heinz had a great fruit juice soft drink long before today's "healthful fruit juices" were popular. It got off to a great start upon expansion from test market. Then, Operations made a few "helpful" technical changes. No other testing was done. Approximately 6-8 weeks after expansion, "bloaters" began to appear at retail.

This product was a complete and expensive screw-up, and never seen again. And Heinz lost an opportunity to be a major player in what is today a very large category.

A human note related to successful market testing.

Involve all key parties as soon as possible; especially Sales. The goodwill and spirit of every functional area of a business is required for any successful business initiative.

I hope you've found all this helpful.

These are some of the things to keep in mind as you work to integrate Consumer Insight into your Business Plan, your Advertising Strategy and, finally, to seek that ultimate Consumer Insight experience– the Market Test– where all our sophisticated thinking and meeting room theatrics are exposed to the burning light of reality.

Do your job well, with a genuine concern for communicating with your consumers, and that light will shine on your achievements– and both you and your company will benefit.

One final tip from an old hand.

Give your agency a lot of your product. A lot of it. And make sure they use it.

This should be particularly aimed at "the creatives."

There are two reasons for this. One was well-covered by Lisa– familiarizing yourself with the product, treating yourself as a consumer.

But there's another reason. And remember, as a Brand Manager your agency is a very specialized target consumer that must also be managed with insight.

The reason you want your product to be in your agency's life- with their family, their neighbors and relatives- is to make sure that they *believe in it!*

This goes beyond professionalism and right to the heart of the way we are as human beings.

And as I see the truly bright, dedicated and hard-working young professionals in Brand Management, I am more convinced than ever that management of this human dimension is the critical differentiating factor.

Today, most Brand Managers have very similar backgrounds and resources. All have essentially the same computer print-outs, the same sales forces, the same sources of information, and the same advertising agencies.

Certainly, your brands and budgets might be different- but I've seen miracles in marketing seemingly done with no more than mirrors, as it were- and entirely too many well-funded disasters.

What distinguishes the big winners in the marketplace? Very simply, **it is insights translated into actions.**

And that is something every individual in Brand Management can commit to- whatever your responsibility, whatever your brand.

Here in Oregon, there's a smart shoe company down the road and they've got themselves a smart agency.

It's always been interesting to me how the smart players seem to end up working with each other.

They make a good shoe- but, then again, so do a lot of their competitors.

The key differentiating factor has been their ability to translate meaningful insights into meaningful actions in the marketplace.

And the message from my friends and neighbors at NIKE is my message to you– "Just do it."

Robb Bell is President of the Mt. Hood Group, in Hood River, OR — a business consulting company providing a complete range of services. Mr. Bell also conducts seminars for Marketing Management in Marketing and Advertising Evaluation - which provided the source material for his article.

Mr. Bell began his career at the Procter & Gamble Company, where he became the youngest Group Product Manager in the history of the company. He moved to Heinz at age 29 as Marketing Director and supervised a rejuvenation of the USA Division's business. The team doubled sales, tripled profits, and quadrupled ROI in 3 1/2 years.

He also worked at MCA (Marketing Corporation of America) before founding the Mt. Hood Group.

22 INSIGHT IN THE CLASSROOM

by Stu Hyatt, Assistant Professor
Newhouse School of Public Communications,
Syracuse University

When I started in advertising, I'm afraid that the consumer wasn't always a top-of-mind consideration. But the fact is they didn't really have to be. There was less competition, less media, less clutter and many more unmet needs. There were mass produced products, mass markets and mass media– each offering exciting new opportunities and a receptive audience for your message.

Today, however, we're all looking at mature markets, brand proliferation, media fragmentation, niche markets, perceived parity, brand erosion, consumer convergence and a lot more. Today, if you're not prepared to do a good bit of thinking about just what being "consumer-driven" means, you've got a tough road ahead of you. In fact, you've got a tough road ahead of you even if you do understand it.

And teaching students to understand consumers is one of the major activities in my classes in the Newhouse School at Syracuse University.

At the first meeting of my advertising copywriting class I'll usually screen a reel of commercials, none of which have any "copy." Then I ask what the copywriters did to help make them better commercials. We spend an hour or so discussing the fact that most good copywriters spend more of their time thinking than writing.

Of course, the question is– thinking about *what?* Well, the product, of course. Most copywriters have a pretty good idea about how to do that. (And, if they don't, there are always plenty of account executives and clients to help your thinking along.)

But how do you think about the consumer? After all, that's really the place where your message has to play– inside the mind of the consumer. This is a tremendous challenge for young writers with developing skills.

I was particularly pleased to discover Lisa's book, because it contained a great deal of what I think about the subject in one thoughtful, logically organized, accessible place. And it's become part of both my copywriting and graduate level Integrated Marketing Communications (IMC) classes.

While the issues of integrated marketing and copywriting are in many ways diverse, there is no doubt in my mind that anyone anticipating a career that depends on informed marketing decisions, had better learn to get in touch with today's consumer.

And this job will get tougher. The more data the Information Age spews out, the more markets fragment, the more messages compete for consumer's attention, the more difficult the job will become.

But here's the good news– as the task becomes more difficult, the need will grow for people who can turn data and information into insight and inspiration.

While I believe that advertising today can no longer ram "ring around the collar" down the consumer's throat, I also believe that consumers will still occasionally reach out and grab an ad or commercial and "participate" in it.

Howard Gossage said, "People read what interests them. Sometimes it's an ad." Someone at BBDO said, "The right

211

product image must be seamlessly joined with the right 'you' image." Weiden & Kennedy talks about "personalized truth."

All of the above, it seems to me, are talking about the things generated by Consumer Insight.

Even some classic campaigns, renowned for their cleverness, were actually based on important Consumer Insights. Paula Green, one of the creators of the Avis "We Try Harder" campaign, suggested that many people missed the real strength of the work. The target (commonly a sales person on the road), was generally in the same position as Avis- working hard to out-hustle a bigger competitor. These people identified with the Avis message *because they lived it!* They tried harder. And that's why the campaign hit their Sweet Spot.

Lisa has provided several good exercises in her book. Unfortunately, in our class there isn't time to do them all. But here are the three types of exercises I use to help students begin developing their consumer "antennae."

Stage One. "One to One."

First I use the exercise comprised of simply writing home for money. (Something most students are doing a lot anyway.) In this deceptively simple assignment you can really focus on the dynamics of one-to-one communication that is so critical.

It's a good assignment because in virtually every case, these letters produce strong elements of emotional, persuasive communications and bring home the point that Consumer Insight into the target (mom and dad), combined with knowledge of the product (the son or daughter), often results in a seamless union of the product to the target.

This same equation will work equally well against other targets and products. It's an excellent exercise for learning to think of advertising as a one-on-one communication. And it sets a standard.

You should then try for that level of empathy, understanding and persuasion in all of your assignments.

Stage Two. Learn to Know People "Just Like You."

Next we do an exercise where we can do some interviewing and some segmentation. The assignments vary, but I try to design a project where our "consumers" are students here at Syracuse.

For example, we have a good sample of a target audience if our project is recruiting high school students for S.U.

The assignment is to develop advertising with the objective of getting high school seniors to put Syracuse on their short list of colleges and universities they would like to consider.

We work at defining the S.U. brand image, as well as a brand equity inventory and evaluation. Then, each student must interview six freshmen for input on what they considered in choosing a school. Based on those findings and the brand review, we collectively develop three concepts which, in turn, we test with representatives of the target (S.U. Freshmen) in both one-on-ones and focus groups. (Naturally, high-school seniors who haven't made a decision yet would be even better.)

We begin by discovering segmentation. For example, there's a group of students who chose Syracuse *because of Newhouse*. They wouldn't be here if Newhouse weren't here. This segment has a pretty good idea of what they want to do. The same is true for students who come to S.U. for the Maxwell School, the Management School, the College of Visual & Performing Arts, and the Architecture School.

Then there's the segment who, in a great majority, choose the S.U. College of Arts & Sciences because they *don't know*

213

what they want to do. That's just the beginning. We discover segments and test concepts and hypotheses.

The key is to develop an exercise where it's possible to do the necessary interviewing with your fellow students. Then as you "learn how to learn," you'll know the process and the feelings that go with discovering the segments and developing consumer insights.

Stage Three. Learn to Know People "Not Like Me."
Then, we move to another exercise, where the student is *not* the target.

Simply understanding on a gut level that *we are not the target audience* is one of the most critical steps in learning to communicate with them. *Eg.- Assumption that Snapple sales declined due to [perceived] fattiness.*

Until we begin to understand who that target really is, we're flying blind trying to reach them, let alone persuade them. Too often, we end up relying on "how it feels" to us, or the art director in the next office.

An example of a good exercise might be something in the health care industry, or anything else with a target group over 50.

The most readily available data base is myself and several colleagues in the AARP Generation. The assignment is to develop concepts for one-on-one interviews and focus groups – and here I can be the one targetted and interviewed. I also do the grading– but that's exactly like the real world where target consumers "grade" your work.

Chances are, the students' parents are also in the target. I've found they enjoy being involved in school work, particularly when it's not asking for money (such as the earlier assignment).

It becomes clear to each person in the class that they don't look on aches and pains the same way a gray panther does.

So far, this exercise seems to demonstrate that the target is much more interested in benefits than being reminded of aches and pains or other dramatizations of "the problem."

Learning how to get to know consumers very different from you at this early stage gives you a great head start in any type of communication. *Eg. Blacks' higher breakfast meat consumption — it's an important meal.*

This is a particularly important lesson to learn as you're developing your skills. Too often, you end up testing your ideas out on your peers and on teachers who are used to dealing with a student's point-of-view.

What happens is you develop your skills, without integrating the process of learning to understand your audience.

Then, at a later stage, getting to know someone different becomes an inconvenience for writers who have learned to write for themselves.

Not surprisingly, this is a problem throughout the industry and at the root of many complaints about talent "more interested in awards than sales."

That's why developing these habits can be tremendously helpful in developing the right mindset for the career that awaits. Don't wait. Start now.

As career opportunities expand into what we call Integrated Marketing Communications, and whatever new variations emerge in this increasingly fast-paced world, becoming adept at developing a consumer focus and those all-important Consumer Insights will be even more critical. For example, in "IMC," the whole communications strategy is designed around the target.

It's literally impossible to develop a strategy without understanding your target. In earlier days, a knowledge of the product and a general demographic description of the target was enough. Not any more.

This is all part of a total reordering of the marketing communications industry. And there is a corresponding reordering of the curriculum of learning institutions, like Syracuse, as we work to offer realistic preparation for careers in this changing industry.

If I may predict the future, even though the present seems unclear, many of the new career opportunities in a wide variety of disciplines will be based on some form of consumer insight. IMC, Account Planning, media planning, the creative aspect of all forms of marketing communications, new media forms and delivery mechanisms...each of these will demand an ability to generate and/or respond to Consumer Insights. It will become a key part of the job description.

It will be those who understand and prepare themselves for this consumer-driven shift who will be the sought-after candidates for tomorrow's careers. And this little book is a great foundation. Thanks, Lisa.

Stu Hyatt spent 30 years in the advertising business. He has served as Management Supervisor, Director of Corporate Communications and Client. But mostly, he has worked as a copywriter/Creative Director at Delahanty Kurnit & Geller, Young and Rubicam, BBDO, J. Walter Thompson and Doyle Dane Bernbach.

Currently he is an Assistant Professor at the Newhouse School of Public Communications at Syracuse University. He teaches both the creative process and the strategic planning aspects of integrated marketing communications.

23 MIS AND THE INSIGHT FRONTIER

By Jean Luber
Coopers & Lybrand

A lot of words start with "MIS." Mistake. Misanthrope. Misinformation. Misery. So when I have to explain "MIS," I'm often starting off on the wrong foot.

Actually, MIS stands for Management Information Systems.

And that's what I help my clients work with every day.

Lisa's book talks about the progression of DATA to IN-FORMATION to INSIGHT to INSPIRATION. I'd like to tell you a bit about MIS's evolution in the first part of that process– turning DATA into usable INFORMATION.

It's additionally important in that the real breakthrough in MIS wasn't so much technical as it was conceptual- shifting from managing information to providing information to management. It's still called MIS, but it's become a very different field.

I also want to address our latest challenge– adding insight to your information.

And I'll try not to be boring. Okay?

Ultimately, MIS deals with how to get information to management in a way that helps them make better business decisions.

Yet, Management Information System departments have been the bane of many companies. Mention computers and

217

it conjures up images of strange people, with slide rulers and pocket protectors, who speak in even stranger tongues. But, today, computer technology touches everyone's life. Daily real-life examples include bank automated teller machines, credit card approval processing, cash registers, and your own microwave oven. And managing this information is particularly important to those who manage.

In the beginning, computer systems were large, inaccessible, expensive and used for voluminous number crunching. Major users of MIS were primarily banks and insurance companies. The systems were used as large calculators- and the systems produced reams of DATA. The data was used by clerks to perform their jobs faster. An investment in systems was used to offset an investment in personnel.

CEOs, CFOs, and company directors never saw any of this data in its original format. The data was "massaged" and reviewed by operating departments such as accounting, tax and sales. Data was reduced to a few key business indicators- information- that executives could review and then use as input in their decisions.

However, the information obtained was not timely. Typically, preparing key operating statements took fifteen to thirty days- often longer. Executives could use this information to see what had gone wrong. But for day-to-day operating decisions, they still had to use the traditional management tools of experience and common sense. And, of course, "projections," which are like guesses- only you get nice-looking charts to show what your guess looks like.

The major turning point came with the major advances in microchip technology and the advent of Personal Computers (PC's) in the 1980's. Computer manufacturers like Apple made technology accessible. They even made it seem like fun. Others, like IBM, made PC's acceptable to management.

Manufacturers such as NCR changed their cash registers from calculators to computers.

Suddenly, there was more data then ever. Universal Product Code (UPC) and Electronic Data Interchange (EDI) produced more important data, faster than ever.

Meanwhile, management wanted to use that data. They wanted the systems in their companies to be as accessible and as easy to use as the Apple PCs. Executives who had never been interested in application system development were suddenly asking the MIS department PC-type questions - like whether their computers had enough RAM. This makes MIS people laugh (guess we do have a strange sense of humor).

But management wasn't smiling. They looked at the investment they had in technology the millions of dollars spent on large systems projects – and wondered what benefit they were obtaining.

Did the systems they had help them with their day-to-day operating decisions? No. The information measured their performance historically with month-to-date and year-to-date totals. It was still a "rear-view mirror." In addition, executives wondered why their company's MIS departments couldn't deliver system applications more quickly. As they saw PC based software growing in profusion, some wondered why the traditional IBM mainframe applications weren't as easy to use as the Apple Macintosh in the TV commercials. (Whether or not Apple's computers penetrated corporate America in a major way, their message had great impact).

Most of all, they didn't want to wade through increasingly large piles of computer print-outs to get the information they needed.

The result was an evolutionary, even revolutionary shift– from MIS being technology-driven and managing information to being customer-driven and providing information to management.

This shift is still going on. Different companies are at varying stages of this evolution and so are MIS people.

But the major characteristic has been a shift to a consumer focus- in this case, the consumer is management.

In most instances, this has meant another set of initials- EIS - Executive Information Systems.

Executive Information Systems were developed as a result of the need of busy management to view critical information on a timely (sometimes daily) basis, as well as to model future business trends the same way they'd manipulate a spreadsheet. EIS also provided executives with a user friendly PC-type environment. For example, many of these systems allow end users to:

• Do key word searches on major business publications such as the Wall Street Journal.

• Chart and graph business trends for easy viewing of trend information.

• Highlight favorable/unfavorable business variances by user-defined criteria such as product line, operating division or customer.

• Trade key performance indicators.

With EIS, we've finally managed to translate *data* into *information* in a meaningful way.

Naturally, MIS departments have found that, as a result of new technology such as PC's and EIS applications, delivery expectations have increased. Another Consumer Insight– once management gets used to getting good information, they want more of it.

Executives no longer expect to receive operating statements 15 days after month end close- they want key information at their fingertips on a timely basis. Usually immediately.

Quite simply, MIS found that it needed to become client service oriented. Executives wanted *information* organized in a logical (to them) fashion that would provide *insight* into their business. And MIS responded to that need.

Executives, in turn, have become better at using this information to respond and react to competition in the marketplace. MIS organizations have also found that the executives are more closely monitoring and measuring their technology investment in terms of tools executives can use.

Just as in the world of marketing, the product is being re-designed to meet the need of the customer.

But, of course, the evolution is still in process.

If you're an executive (or an MIS person) involved in these decisions, here are some basic questions to ask:

1. Can I get a "snapshot?"

We try to apply "The five-minute rule." Does your information (or your presentation) get to the point in the first five minutes? If not, you're still not getting information to management; you're just managing information.

2. Can I focus in on problem areas?

Naturally, this also means that your "snapshot" can highlight those areas. And it means that your system can respond to management questions. But you should be able to shift easily into a more detailed level of information.

3. Can I see past the loading dock?

This is the next revolution in MIS. It's one we're all wrestling with- trying to add "antennae" to our systems to see beyond the transaction and into the customer relationship. For one of my clients, we're working hard to develop systems that collect information about end-users, even though our sale is to distributors.

One insurance company is using their system as a business development tool to update valuations of insured property.

Upgrading customer service is another critical area. Ask yourself- what happens when one of your customers calls your company? How well does your system respond?

Today, many consumer product companies are revising their business applications to help them service their customers better. They want their client service representatives to have information at their fingertips about the customers' orders, shipping preferences, and billing information. They don't want to lose customers because the customer was transferred to ten departments and no one in those departments seemed to know how to help them.

In today's market, the value of an existing customer is greater than ever. MIS should be a valuable tool in measuring and, ultimately, improving that relationship.

For MIS, this is the INSIGHT frontier, where we design systems that help management see deeper into their relationship with their consumers.

And, of course, you should also be using *external* MIS systems.

Today, most internal MIS organizations can provide management with a solid base of information about their customers, products and sales trends. However, this does not provide management with a total picture about their customers and ultimate end-users.

Organizations like IRI and A. C. Nielson provide important information about the ultimate consumer of a product. These companies use surveys and systems targeted at the end-users. They also help you keep track of your competition and the category.

Combined with your internal MIS systems, you now have the tools to make immediate evaluations, shorten response time and more quickly and accurately measure results. You now are dealing with information in a way that encourages better insight.

The need for Consumer Insight is having an important impact on all the people involved with your company's information– your MIS people.

First, it has been the basis of the shift from managing information to providing information to management.

Second, it is the driving force in the search for new ways to extend your company's vision into your relationship with your customers.

To do this, you need exceptional people in your MIS department– just as you want exceptional people in all your departments.

Clients ask me– how do I tell the difference? (Remember, we're strange people who speak a strange language).

The answer is really quite simple.

The best MIS people can talk to you like a real person. All that technology is just a tool to get you what you need.

The worst MIS people are still trapped in technologies and "obscure logic paths." The technology is a wall keeping you from what you need.

In short, the best MIS person says, "yes," and the worst says, "no."

It's not strange people speaking a strange language at all—it's real people opening a vital window of information into the operations of your company.

And I hope that as your own systems develop, they help deliver the INFORMATION and INSIGHTS you need to make the best decisions for your company.

The INSPIRATION, of course, is up to you.

But we're working on it.

Jean Luber is Managing Associate for Coopers & Lybrand, specializing in Management Consulting Services and Information Technology.

24 INSIGHT AND SALESMANSHIP

by Maynard Grossman
vp Operations and Sales
WGCI-FM, Chicago

Sales is an area where insight is critical. As Lisa's book mentions, Consumer Insight is part of some of the earliest principles of salesmanship.

This article is based on the kind of advice I give beginning sales people who work for me. It's about the kind of insights you need to develop to sell successfully.

Too many people have a view that sales is some sort of fast-talking attempt to dominate a relationship– nothing could be farther from the truth.

Selling is about insight. It's about the insights you offer and the insights you develop.

I'm going to talk about radio sales, which is my specialty, but variations on those principles should be helpful to you in many sales functions, particularly in media sales.

The first insight is this– don't be a salesperson. A salesperson is viewed as someone who wants to sell you something. Your customer has no interest in another salesperson in his or her life. (Unless, of course, they already want what you're selling, in which case you're an order taker.)

You want to become a marketing resource– and, when you boil that down to its essence, the primary thing you are offering as a marketing resource is…insight. Because insights are the foundation of connecting with your customer.

We're going to talk about how to get those insights.

First, we'll talk about the two groups of consumers you must develop insights into– your potential clients and your stations's audience– and the way you have to make connections between the two.

My variation on Lisa's Sweet Spot formula is:

Audience Insight + Advertiser Insight = Sweet Spot.

Second, we'll talk about ways we can move from Data and Information to Insight and Inspiration.

Third, I'd like to talk about some interviewing approaches we use in our business.

Fourth, I'd like to talk about some of the kinds of inspirations that can come about when we start to think of ourselves as a consumer-focused marketing resource rather than as a sales force.

1. Getting to Know Your Customers.

Selling media, particularly radio, demands that you have solid insight into two kinds of customers:

A. Your stations' audience

B. Clients and potential clients – advertisers.

To do your job well, you must be able to identify the right potential advertisers for your station's audience and then provide insights into your station's audience to those potential advertisers.

Right now, without knowing a single one of them, I'll tell you what most of those potential advertisers are dealing with– dozens of media representatives: up to 40 radio stations, 3 or 4 outdoor companies, 5 or 6 TV stations, some newspapers, magazines, cable and probably someone selling ball point pens, balloons, T-shirts and bumper stickers.

Key decision makers have only so much time.

And that means the first thing they must do is eliminate those who can't do anything for them. So don't just stand there with your foot in the door, figure out what you can do for them.

The first thing you have to do is understand your station's audience so that you can determine the best prospects based on your ability to meet their needs. Those are the key decision-makers that you should focus on.

You are not selling time or space. You are selling an opportunity for a marketer to effectively connect with your station's audience. Your first job is to determine the best possible connections.

So let's talk about how to develop an in-depth insight into your station's audience.

2. Data/Information/Insight– Understanding Your Station's Audience.

Our industry provides a lot of data and information about our audiences. It's up to you to provide the insight.

We have resources that will tell us about our audience's consumption patterns as well as give us additional demographic and lifestyle information. And radio stations have a further advantage in that our audiences tend to be more segmented. It's easier for us to get to know our audience than broader media vehicles, like TV and newspapers.

To understand what's special about your segment, you have to learn how to use the secondary research that's available. In our industry, there's Burch Qualiscan, Impact Resources' "Mart Data," and International Demographics' "Media Audit" as well as MediaMark (MRI) and Simmons Market Research Bureau data.

You have to learn how to extract the information and insights you need. There's a lot to work with, including: age, income, ethnicity, job, residence, lifestyle, preferred leisure activity, product usage and intent to purchase.

For example, you can find market by market product usage information combined with demographic information and all of this cross-tabbed with media usage.

As you analyze the data, look for the strongest product categories for your station–you want to focus on medium to heavy users.

You may find yourself pleasantly surprised by the product categories where your station's audience is a prime target.

Now you're starting to be able to move into the area of providing insight to potential clients. Let's say one of them is a fairly strong newspaper advertiser and you have information that shows that your station has a fairly high index of heavy users.

You also find some cross-tabbed data that shows that they are not particularly heavy newspaper readers.

Now you're starting to become a market resource offering insight– not merely one more vendor looking for a purchase order. This insight into your audience is a legitimate reason for making a presentation to that advertiser.

Another area that might contain insight lies in regional differences for your market. Here's an example, a recent presentation to a health care marketer.

Nationally, hospital outpatient care and clinic usage indicated the target should be women 25 to 54. This was not our station's strongest demographic.

But we found some recent research that gave us a break-out for the Chicago market. The Chicago market, on the average, skews younger. When we looked at a regional breakout of this information it showed that the core of the market was 25 to 44, with an important secondary market not older, but younger, 18 to 24. This was an excellent fit with our audience profile.

We brought this to the marketer's attention. They were pleased to have insights that allowed them to make more informed marketing decisions in our market.

It was a marketing presentation, not a sales call. But it's not surprising that they added our station to their list.

Connecting your audience with potential advertisers often demands more than presenting numbers.

Our station is "urban contemporary." One third of our audience is white. Two thirds isn't. Connecting predominantly white decision-makers to this audience can take more than a mere recitation of product usage information.

We recently took a foreign car marketing executive on a short consumer excursion. We went down to one of the main parking garages and helped him count the foreign cars (his model and competitors') driven to work by our audience.

We dramatized what we were saying with a little reality reinforcement. We helped the marketers focus on their market, which was our audience.

We didn't sell, we educated. We provided insight.

3. Identifying (& Understanding) Client Needs.

Now let's talk about how to develop additional insight into our potential advertisers. Our secondary research helps us focus on categories. Now we have to develop insights into the needs of individual marketers.

Even in the same category, the needs of different marketers may be dramatically different. Basically, you want to do what we call a Needs Analysis.

There are some nice tools we can use for this. One of my

favorites is an interview format developed by the Radio Advertising Bureau. It's "The Consultant Interview." It helps you ask the right questions to learn an advertiser's needs.

It starts with "pre-appointment research" where, among other things, you visit the store and/or interview a few customers. Then it helps you structure your interview with the client. It includes Consumer Insight questions like "In what ways do your competitors' customers differ from yours?" "Who are your typical customers?" and "What other customers would you like to attract?"

If it's a retailer with multiple locations, you may also want to find out if he has different types of customers at different locations, as is often the case. As a result, you may find that your station's audience will be particularly important for some of his locations.

This interviewing process can help you develop the insights, and maybe even the inspirations, that will help you become a marketing partner and not just another vendor waiting in the lobby.

Naturally, once you discover the client's needs, you may have to do a little work to find the answer for those needs– you may even need a little inspiration.

A number of years ago, when I was working in Washington, a friend and I pitched the area's finest furniture store. We had determined that, while he had a relatively good business with well-to-do Washingtonians, he really didn't have anything in the way of a business plan. That was his need. And it was going to be very hard to get him on any track until he did one.

We got information from The National Home Furnishings Association, including how furniture marketers should prepare a business plan, and basic research on the industry: customer types, seasonality and other category information.

We met with him, took him through the material and helped him develop a basic business plan. He was delighted. I placed the radio and my friend handled the print.

It happened because we focused first and foremost on understanding the client's needs.

Well, you might ask, "Isn't that a lot of work– writing up a business plan just to sell a few radio ads– and don't I just want to make a sale?"

To that question I would offer these insights.

First, if you're not presenting logical and useful information designed to help the client's needs, chances are your presentation won't be very strong. In this competitive marketplace, it's doubtful you'll be successful.

Second, even if you're successful in making the sale the first time, you've got problems. Since it wasn't based on meeting the client's needs in the first place, chances are the program won't be all that successful. Remember, you can't build your business just making that first sale over and over– you need to build repeat business, or what I call "residual business." Whatever you call it, it depends on satisfied customers.

Actually I don't mind a bit if you take that approach – it means less competition for me.

Most media sales people are carnivores fighting over the same carcass. I can't tell you how much time is spent with sales people going out and basically telling clients they spent their money on the wrong media. The result is "cannibalization." All that time and energy is spent fighting over existing (and often already spent) dollars rather than developing new business.

In addition, if you've been selling based on insight into the client's marketing needs, when the other media people come calling (as surely they will), to tell your client that he spent his money on the wrong media, your relationship will be stronger because it was based on meeting his needs, not yours. And because it was based on connecting your audience with his business.

4. Building Business with Inspirations.
You're supposed to be a marketing partner.

A marketing partner goes from insight to inspiration, every once in a while. And so should you.

In our business, inspirations tend to be smart connections, and we can often use them more than once.

We showed suburban drug stores that our "urban contemporary" listeners did a lot of shopping in their stores.

I also brought this marketing information to the attention of other suburban retailers. As I recall, we signed up a chain of auto parts stores as well.

In radio, we have a name for a certain type of inspiration that hits Sweet Spots all over the place–*Promotions.*

I'm going to fiddle with Lisa's equation one more time, and offer you a variation that explains what a lot of our promotions are all about.

Client Need + Client Need = Promotion

Let me give you an example.

The Marketing Director of an arena had extra capacity for a number of sporting events. We told him that we knew what he could do with his spare tickets– give them to us.

Then, we told a Sporting Goods Marketer that we had a way for him to generate more traffic– give away tickets to this particular sporting event.

We developed a program that met everyone's needs. And

our audience responded because it was a darn good deal for them as well– make a purchase at the sporting goods store and get either two FREE tickets or, if the purchase was smaller, a-two-tickets-for-the-price-of-one coupon.

It meant extra traffic for the sporting goods store, extra income from parking and concessions for the arena and extra income for us. After all, a deal that good needs to be advertised.

Here, we had insights into the needs of two marketers and connected them to build a promotion that hit everyone's Sweet Spot.

Working like this is a lot of fun.

You add value with insight. You become a marketing partner who is valued as a resource and brought into the planning process instead of a vendor forced to compete on price and wait in the lobby.

Your programs work better because they're based on insights. Your relationships last longer because they're based on meeting needs.

Your job is to connect insights into your audience with insights into your clients' needs. Simply put, your job is to hit Sweet Spots.

Maynard Grossman is vp of Operations and Sales at WGCI-FM, Chicago's top-rated music station.

He was cited as one of the best Sales Managers in the U.S. by the Radio Advertising Bureau.

25 INSIGHT AT NIGHT

With Mike Miller, Owner, Biddy Mulligan's

In June of 1990, Mike Miller left his job as an Account Director on P&G at Leo Burnett and bought the legendary Chicago night club, Biddy Mulligan's. We talked with him about how he applied principles of Consumer Insight to a unique retail business.

What insights do you have into your motivations for leaving a leading ad agency to own your own business?

It's always been important to me to be able to translate my insights and inspirations into actions. And when you run your own business, you have a chance to do that every day.

I loved working at Leo Burnett– it's a great agency and they really gave me an opportunity to do my best and work with terrific people.

During the last 3-5 years I was there, the principles in Lisa's book were being applied with increasing interest and effectiveness. But this isn't just something for a large marketer– it's important that the owner of a small business develops consumer insights and acts upon them.

I tend to have strong convictions about my insights - and I think that was my primary motivation for wanting to run my own business. I wanted control, a chance to do it, without spending all the time and effort that's necessary in a large organization to sell it up the line.

I think most people who run their own businesses are looking for the satisfaction of putting their insights and inspirations to work immediately.

Tell us about the business you bought.

Biddy Mulligan's is a unique club. It's been around twenty years and was one of the very first "showcase" rock clubs, where you could come hear a "name" group in a club setting. Twenty years later, it's still an important venue both for new groups looking to get established, and somewhat well-known groups that can't fill a really large concert hall.

However, in many ways, Biddy's was a "mature brand." It wasn't new any more. There was a lot more competition. Once there were 6 or 7 "showcase" clubs– now there are dozens.

And, while business was okay, it was on the edge of decline – with some fairly serious problems. First, it was out-of-the-way and parking was terrible. I've mentioned the increased competition. Most important, *there wasn't any regular business!* People came for the names. Period.

From the surly greeting at the door to the warm beer, an evening at Biddy's wasn't what it could be. Nobody said, "Let's go to Biddy's." They said, "Let's go hear so and so." The brutal fact was, nobody came 'cause they liked the place. As a result, it was only open 3 nights a week. If there wasn't a name group booked, there wasn't any business.

We had to revitalize a mature brand with consumer insight.

How did you start?

I began by learning to think like one of my customers.

There was a 6-8 week period before I took over. I used that time to see it as a customer. I went almost every night. I looked, I listened and I learned.

This included observing a lot of what was communicated by body language. And, of course, I did a bit of "Ethnography."

It was a process similar to viewing from behind a focus group one-way mirror. So when we took over, I already knew

235

a lot of what we had to do to improve our product.

What was that?

As I saw it, the components we could control consistently were: the quality of the sound, the product we served–primarily beer, and the way people were treated.

First, we re-did the sound system. Sound is a function of a lot of things– the reflectiveness of the walls, the quality of the electronics and the placement of the speakers. Like Lisa's book says, we already know a lot. While I wasn't an audio expert, I knew what I liked.

I believe music is a basic human experience, and that basic human feeling of being part of the music and wanting to dance is what Biddy's is all about.

Our objective was to generate the most memorable musical experience we could. We turned a noisy bar into something almost like a sound studio. It wasn't cheap–we estimate that we spend about a dollar per customer per night to make sure the sound is the best it can be.

We wanted an audio product that was clean and crisp– not the loudest–just the best. For example, if you ever walk into a club with a live band, one of the first things you'll hear is a soft, or not-so-soft, low buzzing. It comes from improper grounding– and it's not easy to get that buzz out of a system. Particularly since different groups generate different sounds with different equipment. In most places, you just get used to it, but it's really a low-level irritant that gets in the way of your enjoying the music. Here, it's gone. Totally.

We don't want people to notice a single negative that can get in the way of their enjoyment.

Our other product is, frankly, alcohol– primarily beer. We think it's also part of man's nature and history. It doesn't seem to be asking too much that it be something we do well.

The previous operation had an old air-cooled tap-line and a basement cooler where people would carry up a few cases of beer and put them on the floor. This place can get up to 95°. The result was warm beer.

Beer companies work hard to put out a good-tasting product. We wanted to deliver the best experience possible with that product– clean, fresh and cold. So we invested in a new high-tech tap line and bottle coolers. The results were practically immediate.

We work to maintain that quality, too. Our tap lines are cleaned twice a month– most bars clean theirs twice a year. I shudder to think when the old lines were last cleaned.

Incidentally, we found some "consumer detectives" who were very helpful– the guys who drive the beer trucks. They had quite a bit of valuable information to share with us.

The final part of our product was how we treated people. The previous operation was strictly a showroom. There were no customer relationships, and little regard for anything but the customers' money.

We changed that. And we pretty much changed it with the people we already had. We kept reinforcing the importance of being nice to the customer. We made it clear that we believed it was important, and we kept people focused on it.

We run what is called a "speed bar," it's not one where you sit and talk to the bartender– we work to get it out fast so you can go back to your friends and enjoy the show. Well, even though we were running a speed bar, our bartenders started to realize that being pleasant was paying off– in more tips and more regulars– people who would regularly sit at their station. They'd never seen that before– and it was key to our basic objective of developing a regular repeat customer base for Biddy's. Our philosophy was "Make a friend a night." (We're open 250-300 nights a year.)

So, we fixed our product, based on initial brand insights that came, quite simply, from thinking like a customer. Our next step was getting to know them.

How did you get to know your customers?

Just like in Lisa's book, we had to move from DATA to INFORMATION, and then to INSIGHTS.

There were no supplier lists, no customer data base to speak of...nothing. So we built up our data base from every source we could get our hands on.

We had a lot of "audiences" we needed to be in touch with:

• Our customers– more on this later.

• Music suppliers– such as booking agents, managers, performers, and record company executives– this was a critical early audience.

• The press– primarily newspapers and radio stations.

• Our suppliers– sound companies, electricians and other trades people that provide services and equipment.

For a small business, a well-maintained data-base program can be a core part of your customer relationship program. First, it's pretty easy to know who your customers are– they come in your door– and it's relatively easy to get their names and addresses.

For the mass consumer brands I worked on, like Cheer, this wasn't really possible or cost-effective. For a local business it's very do-able.

Well, we started building the list and we've kept working it. Today, we have a data base of 3,000 names.

What did you do with it?

First, we let the music industry know Biddy's was under

new management. We wanted to hear from them. We built our list from every source we could find. The result was a new level of activity and interest.

Second, we got the name of every customer that walked in our door. We worked to build relationships with customers where none existed before.This is in addition to the in-club experience. Remember, Biddy's is still a destination and even with our "regulars," we believe we have to keep recruiting them and rewarding them for being regulars.

Who are these "regulars?"

A good question. I can answer it because we did a bit of segmentation. We have two major consumer segments, one minor segment and two other small but important audiences. Defining these really helps us focus on what to do.

The two major segments are:

1. "Dead Heads." It's a positive term and one they use themselves. They're the hippies of the '90s. They range from late teens (naturally they have to be 21 to get into Biddy's) into their early fifties. They're our primary customer.

They have a lot of shared values, they care about the world, they're mellow– not a bunch of high powered young execs in business suits– and music is a big part of their lives.

We work to make Biddy's a welcome spot for them. Even the decor on stage is part of that– colorful African prints that look sort of tie-dyed (The Grateful Dead/"Dead Head" look includes a lot of tie-dyed clothes) and they project what we're about. It's a small thing, but it demonstrates to our customers we're "their kind of people."

2. College Students. This is our second major group. They're critical to achieving the volumes we need– particularly during the week.

We're located between two good-sized universities (Loyola and Northwestern). But, given the age of college students, we only get them for a year or so– then they're gone.

The three other minor, but important, audiences for us:

3. The 30+ "Show Audience." They're irregular. They don't go out much, but will come to hear certain groups. Maybe once or twice a year. In some ways, this is sort of the old Biddy's audience. If we do a good job with our advertising and PR, we'll get them when we feature a group they want to see.

4. The Acts. Particularly local bands. We work to develop a positive relationship with them. Many play for "the door," which helps make it possible for us to achieve our 5 nights a week objective.

5. The Press. It's an even smaller group, but even more critical. A good story or some air play on the radio of a group playing at Biddy's can make our weekend.

Okay, you know your consumers– how do you hit their Sweet Spot?

A lot of the things we do to reach our audiences is driven by a monthly newsletter. For example, the latest– a "Happy Holidays from Your Friends at Biddy Mulligan's" newsletter. The purpose is to build the relationship as well as traffic.

The cover features a Christmas tree design full of logos of bands that played here over the last year. It's also going to be a Christmas ornament we'll give away. It'll be a suprise. It won't cost us much and it's a way we can reward our customers and reinforce the relationship. Think about it. When's the last time you got something free from a club besides a book of matches?

We have a regular series of Customer Appreciation contests. It's our 20th Anniversary– we're giving away a lot of 20 ticket prizes. Bring your friends– have a really good time at Biddy's.

(Even if it's a night when the cover's only $5, this is still a $100 value.)

Those who win are blown away. Again, to get something free from a bar! They're amazed. It builds the relationships and, as you would imagine, fills up the room on our slower nights. Incidentally, we always tell the band when there's an above average number of "house guests."

A lot of clubs send out calendars–but we try to do more than that. We tell them something about the bands we're booking. Remember, music is an important part of their lives– that's a Sweet Spot. Our customers like being knowledgeable–and it shows them we care about the acts we bring into the club.

It pays off in other ways. A reporter just picked up on one of the pieces in this newsletter and wrote a nice feature.We hit his Sweet Spot. It will guarantee more people coming to hear that band for a lot of the right reasons.

To set the right tone, our dog Zeke writes a regular "Zeke the Wonder Dog" column. Again, it projects the right attitude for our customers. And, of course, Zeke has fun writing it.

Month after month, we continue to use this newsletter for relationship building - to make people feel this is their place– and to keep giving them important reasons to come. It hits a lot of Sweet Spots, particularly for that first segment.

What about the college students?

Let me tell you about our major sampling event.

As I mentioned, we needed to develop our college business fresh every school year. I believed that if we could become the place of choice for enough of this group, we'd fill the place five nights a week instead of three.

What was their Sweet Spot?

Very simply, a college student wants a cost-effective good

time. So, we developed a sampling/promotional event to reach those customers and hit that particular Sweet Spot.

The pricing, the timing, even the particular music we featured was designed to hit them right.

The music?

We tried a number of things, but reggae was right for the attitude we wanted to project. It's fun, good-time music. And it's relatively easy to get a good local reggae band.

So, my inspiration (if you want to call it that) was "Reggae Against Recession." It was a 5¢ pitcher of beer (also a $5 cover) My partners thought I was crazy. But it hit a Sweet Spot.

We promote it heavily during the first part of the semester. And it does a lot more than build up a slow night. Students learn where we are, how to get here, where to park, and so on. Most of all, we get a chance to deliver a cost-effective and first-rate entertainment experience.

They hear our sound. They taste our beer. They dance. And, most important, they get treated nice– not like cheapskates taking advantage of a deal.

And the program did exactly what we wanted it to do– develop regular customers who get in the habit of coming to Biddy Mulligan's and having a good time.

It helped us make the transition from being an occasional act-driven destination to becoming a regular place where you'll have a first-rate musical experience.

People who haven't been here in a while say, "This place has changed." They can't put their finger on it. It still looks pretty much the same, but the feeling– the way people are treated, the way people are having a good time– is very different.

How has Consumer Insight made a difference?

There was nothing particularly unique about our objective. Every bar, every club, wants to be a place where people come regularly to have a good time.

The point is, what you have to do to accomplish it. And how you determine what to do in the first place. It all emerges from consumer focus.

Is a 5¢ pitcher of beer an inspiration? Not really and not all by itself. In every business, you can always give it away. But when it's part of an expression of how you want to reach a certain group of consumers with a high degree of impact, based on some insights you already have– you bet it is.

To stay with this simple example, information ranging from when the school year starts, to what kind of live music you can offer on a Tuesday night, is all part of the consumer-driven thinking you bring to bear on your business.

Any other examples?

Here's a cassette tape called "A Taste of Biddy Mulligan's." It's a full length tape, with 14 groups, 14 full-length songs. And it only costs $5.

We're not in the business of selling tapes, we're in the business of building relationships with our customers. Look at how many ways this one tape hits Sweet Spots.

We started by including an order form in a newsletter– a lot of our regulars bought one– and then bought dozens of them as Christmas presents. What a great way to share your favorite place, and your favorite music, with friends– for only $5. At the club, it became a way for our customers to take a memory of their evening home with them.

Among local groups, another important audience for us, many didn't have recording contract yet. It was a great

243

opportunity– we rewarded them. We distributed the tape to radio stations. The press appreciated the role we played in promoting new music here in Chicago and a number of stations gave some of the tunes air play– often with a mention of where you could get the tape.

Most importantly, whether you bought the tape or not, it projected our brand personality. We weren't just there to take customers' money– but we really cared about the music. It was one more way to demonstrate to the consumer what the "new" Biddy Mulligan's was all about.

How else does Consumer Insight help?

When you have that consumer focus, good things tend to happen, even when you don't have large insights. When we took over Biddy's, there was this disgusting back room where stuff had been piled up for years– we cleared it out and cleaned it up. We asked ourselves, what would our customers want? Answer– a pool table.

So, we put in a little area where they could play pool. Not particularly brilliant– but we ended up being pretty smart in ways we hadn't counted on. It drew people to the back room, opened up the front of the club and actually gave us more natural capacity. It gave another focus of activity to the place. That wasn't our plan. It just came from thinking about what our customers might like.

As I said, I think anyone in business for himself is looking for the opportunity to develop insights and then put them to work immediately. Of course, you're not going to be right every time. But with a consumer focus, your learning keeps moving you in the right direction.

How do you feel about marketing alcohol?

We look at ourselves as being primarily in the entertainment business. Alcohol is certainly part of that, but there's a new level of concern among the public and in the market-place. We've responded to that.

In addition to seeing that customers aren't "over-served," which we monitor as best we can, we try to extend that further. If you're going to care about the customer, you don't just take their money and let them stumble out the door. And it's also important to remember that people come for the music. Dealing with a bunch of drunks detracts from that.

We have an extremely good relationship with a particular cab company– we're one of their best customers. We get quick service to help us provide transportation home for anyone who needs it. But, again, you find that as you really focus on your customers' needs, these sorts of solutions can really come pretty easily.

Anything else?

The final point I want to make is to those of you who think you want your own business. If you've never run your own business, I don't think anything prepares you for the amount of work you have to do. You start with energy and inspiration. But there's always so much to do, so much to think about.

If you allow yourself to become exhausted, you won't have the energy or clear-headedness you need to discover those insights and have those inspirations– and act on them.

You have to force yourself to get some rest. You have to learn to delegate.

As an entrepeneur, you have a vision– learn to share it.

A friend bought a business the same time I did. After three months of virtually 24-hour days, I sat down with him and worked to give him some insight into himself. And, some insight into the fact that if he burned himself out, he wouldn't have any business. I hope it helped.

Running my business has been a lot of work– more than I expected. But as an opportunity to develop insights, put them into action and see the results in a very short time, I don't think anything can match it.

And for a final thought?

Whatever business you go into, I wish you well, and I hope that using Consumer Insight as a business tool can contribute to your success as it has to mine.

After graduating from Notre Dame with a bachelor's degree in Business Administration, Mike Miller joined Leo Burnett in 1977. He worked his way up from the Media Department, becoming an account executive on Era and Cheer. He was promoted to Account Director on P&G brands in 1980.

In June of 1990, he left Leo Burnett to own and manage Chicago's legendary blues and rock bar "Biddy Mulligan's." In addition to running the club, Mike is developing a related operation which will organize and promote concerts as well as planning a number of other business ventures.

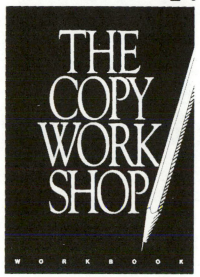
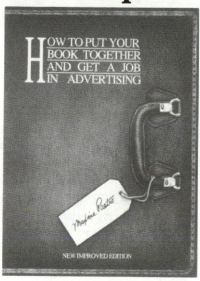

Would You Like
More Consumer Insight?

If you'd like to order more copies of this book, just call or write The Copy Workshop. Seminars featuring the author are also available.

Quantity discounts are available for orders over 5 copies. Libraries may order direct or through Baker & Taylor.

Instructors are encouraged to call us with any questions or suggestions.

Your friends at–

The Copy Workshop

2144 N. Hudson, Chicago, IL 60614
Phone 312-871-1179 • Fax 312-281-4643